Deep Learning for Natural Language Processing

Creating Neural Networks with Python

Palash Goyal

Sumit Pandey

Karan Jain

Apress®

Deep Learning for Natural Language Processing: Creating Neural Networks with Python

Palash Goyal
Bangalore, Karnataka, India

Sumit Pandey
Bangalore, Karnataka, India

Karan Jain
Bangalore, Karnataka, India

ISBN-13 (pbk): 978-1-4842-3684-0
https://doi.org/10.1007/978-1-4842-3685-7

ISBN-13 (electronic): 978-1-4842-3685-7

Library of Congress Control Number: 2018947502

Managing Director, Apress Media LLC: Welmoed Spahr
Acquisitions Editor: Celestin Suresh John
Development Editor: Matthew Moodie
Coordinating Editor: Aditee Mirashi

Cover designed by eStudioCalamar

Cover image designed by Freepik (www.freepik.com)

Distributed to the book trade worldwide by Springer Science+Business Media New York, 233 Spring Street, 6th Floor, New York, NY 10013. Phone 1-800-SPRINGER, fax (201) 348-4505, e-mail orders-ny@springer-sbm.com, or visit www.springeronline.com. Apress Media, LLC is a California LLC and the sole member (owner) is Springer Science+Business Media Finance Inc (SSBM Finance Inc). SSBM Finance Inc is a **Delaware** corporation.

For information on translations, please e-mail rights@apress.com, or visit www.apress.com/rights-permissions.

Apress titles may be purchased in bulk for academic, corporate, or promotional use. eBook versions and licenses are also available for most titles. For more information, reference our Print and eBook Bulk Sales web page at www.apress.com/bulk-sales.

Any source code or other supplementary material referenced by the author in this book is available to readers on GitHub via the book's product page, located at www.apress.com/978-1-4842-3684-0. For more detailed information, please visit www.apress.com/source-code.

Printed on acid-free paper

To our parents, sisters, brothers, and friends
without whom this book would have been
completed one year earlier :)

Table of Contents

About the Authors

Palash Goyal is a senior data scientist and currently works with the applications of data science and deep learning in the online marketing domain. He studied Mathematics and Computing at the Indian Institute of Technology (IIT) Guwahati and proceeded to work in a fast-paced upscale environment.

He has wide experience in E-commerce and travel, insurance, and banking industries. Passionate about mathematics and finance, Palash manages his portfolio of multiple cryptocurrencies and the latest Initial Coin Offerings (ICOs) in his spare time, using deep learning and reinforcement learning techniques for price prediction and portfolio management. He keeps in touch with the latest trends in the data science field and shares these on his personal blog, http://madoverdata.com, and mines articles related to smart farming in free time.

Sumit Pandey is a graduate of IIT Kharagpur. He worked for about a year at AXA Business Services, as a data science consultant. He is currently engaged in launching his own venture.

Karan Jain is a product analyst at Sigtuple, where he works on cutting-edge AI-driven diagnostic products. Previously, he worked as a data scientist at Vitrana Inc., a health care solutions company. He enjoys working in fast-paced environments and at data-first start-ups. In his leisure time, Karan deep-dives into genomics sciences, BCI interfaces, and optogenetics. He recently developed interest in POC devices and nanotechnology for further portable diagnosis. He has a healthy network of 3000+ followers on LinkedIn.

About the Technical Reviewer

Santanu Pattanayak currently works at GE Digital as a staff data scientist and is the author of the deep learning–related book *Pro Deep Learning with TensorFlow—A Mathematical Approach to Advanced Artificial Intelligence in Python*. He has about 12 years of overall work experience, 8 in the data analytics/ data science field, and has a background in development and database technologies.

Prior to joining GE, Santanu worked in such companies as RBS, Capgemini, and IBM. He graduated with a degree in electrical engineering from Jadavpur University, Kolkata, and is an avid math enthusiast. Santanu is currently pursuing a master's degree in data science from IIT Hyderabad. He also devotes his time to data science hackathons and Kaggle competitions, in which he ranks within the top 500 across the globe. Santanu was born and brought up in West Bengal, India, and currently resides in Bangalore, India, with his wife.

Acknowledgments

This work would not have been possible without those who saw us through this book, to all those who believed in us, talked things over, read, wrote, and offered their valuable time throughout the process, and allowed us to use the knowledge that we gained together, be it for proofreading or overall design.

We are especially indebted to Aditee Mirashi, coordinating editor, Apress, Springer Science+Business, who has been a constant support and motivator to complete the task and who worked actively to provide us with valuable suggestions to pursue our goals on time.

We are grateful to Santanu Pattanayak, who went through all the chapters and provided valuable input, giving final shape to the book.

Nobody has been more important to us in the pursuit of this project than our family members. We would like to thank our parents, whose love and guidance are with us in whatever we pursue. Their being our ultimate role models has provided us unending inspiration to start and finish the difficult task of writing and giving shape to our knowledge.

Introduction

This book attempts to simplify and present the concepts of deep learning in a very comprehensive manner, with suitable, full-fledged examples of neural network architectures, such as Recurrent Neural Networks (RNNs) and Sequence to Sequence (seq2seq), for Natural Language Processing (NLP) tasks. The book tries to bridge the gap between the theoretical and the applicable.

It proceeds from the theoretical to the practical in a progressive manner, first by presenting the fundamentals, followed by the underlying mathematics, and, finally, the implementation of relevant examples.

The first three chapters cover the basics of NLP, starting with the most frequently used Python libraries, word vector representation, and then advanced algorithms like neural networks for textual data.

The last two chapters focus entirely on implementation, dealing with sophisticated architectures like RNN, Long Short-Term Memory (LSTM) Networks, Seq2seq, etc., using the widely used Python tools TensorFlow and Keras. We have tried our best to follow a progressive approach, combining all the knowledge gathered to move on to building a question-and-answer system.

The book offers a good starting point for people who want to get started in deep learning, with a focus on NLP.

All the code presented in the book is available on GitHub, in the form of IPython notebooks and scripts, which allows readers to try out these examples and extend them in interesting, personal ways.

CHAPTER 1

Introduction to Natural Language Processing and Deep Learning

Natural language processing (NPL) is an extremely difficult task in computer science. Languages present a wide variety of problems that vary from language to language. Structuring or extracting meaningful information from free text represents a great solution, if done in the right manner. Previously, computer scientists broke a language into its grammatical forms, such as parts of speech, phrases, etc., using complex algorithms. Today, deep learning is a key to performing the same exercises.

This first chapter of *Deep Learning for Natural Language Processing* offers readers the basics of the Python language, NLP, and Deep Learning. First, we cover the beginner-level codes in the Pandas, NumPy, and SciPy libraries. We assume that the user has the initial Python environment (2.x or 3.x) already set up, with these libraries installed. We will also briefly discuss commonly used libraries in NLP, with some basic examples.

© Palash Goyal, Sumit Pandey, Karan Jain 2018
P. Goyal, et al., *Deep Learning for Natural Language Processing*,
https://doi.org/10.1007/978-1-4842-3685-7_1

Finally, we will discuss the concepts behind deep learning and some common frameworks, such as TensorFlow and Keras. Then, in later chapters, we will move on to providing a higher level overview of NLP.

Depending on the machine and version preferences, one can install Python by using the following references:

- `www.python.org/downloads/`

- `www.continuum.io/downloads`

The preceding links and the basic packages installations will provide the user with the environment required for deep learning.

We will be using the following packages to begin. Please refer to the following links, in addition to the package name for your reference:

Python Machine Learning

Pandas (`http://pandas.pydata.org/pandas-docs/stable`)

NumPy (`www.numpy.org`)

SciPy (`www.scipy.org`)

Python Deep Learning

TensorFlow (`http://tensorflow.org/`)

Keras (`https://keras.io/`)

Python Natural Language Processing

Spacy (`https://spacy.io/`)

NLTK (`www.nltk.org/`)

TextBlob (`http://textblob.readthedocs.io/en/dev/`)

We might install other related packages, if required, as we proceed. If you are encountering problems at any stage of the installation, please refer to the following link: `https://packaging.python.org/tutorials/installing-packages/`.

Note   Refer to the Python package index, PyPI (`https://pypi.python.org/pypi`), to search for the latest packages available.

Follow the steps to install pip via `https://pip.pypa.io/en/stable/installing/`.

Python Packages

We will be covering the references to the installation steps and the initial-level coding for the Pandas, NumPy, and SciPy packages. Currently, Python offers versions 2.x and 3.x, with compatible functions for machine learning. We will be making use of Python2.7 and Python3.5, where required. Version 3.5 has been used extensively throughout the chapters of this book.

NumPy

NumPy is used particularly for scientific computing in Python. It is designed to efficiently manipulate large multidimensional arrays of arbitrary records, without sacrificing too much speed for small multidimensional arrays. It could also be used as a multidimensional container for generic data. The ability of NumPy to create arrays of arbitrary type, which also makes NumPy suitable for interfacing with general-purpose data-base applications, makes it one of the most useful libraries you are going to use throughout this book, or thereafter for that matter.

Following are the codes using the NumPy package. Most of the lines of code have been appended with a comment, to make them easier to understand by the user.

Numpy

```
import numpy as np                # Importing the Numpy package
a= np.array([1,4,5,8], float)     # Creating Numpy array with
                                    Float variables
print(type(a))                # Type of variable
> <class 'numpy.ndarray'>

# Operations on the array
a[0] = 5                  #Replacing the first element of the array
print(a)
> [ 5. 4. 5. 8.]

b = np.array([[1,2,3],[4,5,6]], float)   # Creating a 2-D numpy
                                              array
b[0,1]                  # Fetching second element of 1st array
> 2.0

print(b.shape)        #Returns tuple with the shape of array
> (2, 3)

b.dtype               #Returns the type of the value stored
> dtype('float64')

print(len(b))         #Returns length of the first axis
> 2

2 in b                #'in' searches for the element in the array
> True

0 in b
> False
```

```
# Use of 'reshape' : transforms elements from 1-D to 2-D here
c = np.array(range(12), float)
print(c)
print(c.shape)
print('---')
c = c.reshape((2,6))     # reshape the array in the new form
print(c)
print(c.shape)
> [ 0. 1. 2. 3. 4. 5. 6. 7. 8. 9. 10. 11.]
(12,)
---
[[ 0. 1. 2. 3. 4. 5.] [ 6. 7. 8. 9. 10. 11.]]
(2, 6)

c.fill(0)                    #Fills whole array with single value,
                                 done inplace
print(c)
> [[ 0. 0. 0. 0. 0. 0.] [ 0. 0. 0. 0. 0. 0.]]

c.transpose()                #creates transpose of the array, not
                                 done inplace
> array([[ 0., 0.], [ 0., 0.], [ 0., 0.], [ 0., 0.], [ 0., 0.],
[ 0., 0.]])

c.flatten()                  #flattens the whole array, not done
                                 inplace
> array([ 0., 0., 0., 0., 0., 0., 0., 0., 0., 0., 0., 0.])
```

```python
# Concatenation of 2 or more arrays
m = np.array([1,2], float)
n = np.array([3,4,5,6], float)
p = np.concatenate((m,n))
print(p)
> [ 1. 2. 3. 4. 5. 6.]
(6,)

print(p.shape)

# 'newaxis' : to increase the dimensonality of the array
q = np.array([1,2,3], float)
q[:, np.newaxis].shape
> (3, 1)
```

NumPy has other functions, such as zeros, ones, zeros_like, ones_like, identity, eye, which are used to create arrays filled with 0s, 1s, or 0s and 1s for given dimensions.

Addition, subtraction, and multiplication occur on same-size arrays. Multiplication in NumPy is offered as element-wise and not as matrix multiplication. If the arrays do not match in size, the smaller one is repeated to perform the desired operation. Following is an example for this:

```python
a1 = np.array([[1,2],[3,4],[5,6]], float)
a2 = np.array([-1,3], float)
print(a1+a2)
> [[ 0. 5.] [ 2. 7.] [ 4. 9.]]
```

Note   pi and e are included as constants in the NumPy package.

One can refer to the following sources for detailed tutorials on NumPy: www.numpy.org/ and https://docs.scipy.org/doc/numpy-dev/user/ quickstart.html.

NumPy offers few of the functions that are directly applicable on the arrays: sum (summation of elements), prod (product of the elements), mean (mean of the elements), var (variance of the elements), std (standard deviation of the elements), argmin (index of the smallest element in array), argmax (index of the largest element in array), sort (sort the elements), unique (unique elements of the array).

```
a3 = np.array([[0,2],[3,-1],[3,5]], float)
print(a3.mean(axis=0))              # Mean of elements column-wise
> [ 2. 2.]

print(a3.mean(axis=1))              # Mean of elements row-wise
> [ 1. 1. 4.]
```

Note   To perform the preceding operations on a multidimensional array, include the optional argument axis in the command.

NumPy offers functions for testing the values present in the array, such as nonzero (checks for nonzero elements), isnan (checks for "not a number" elements), and isfinite (checks for finite elements). The where function returns an array with the elements satisfying the following conditions:

```
a4 = np.array([1,3,0], float)
np.where(a!=0, 1/a ,a)
> array([ 0.2 , 0.25 , 0.2 , 0.125])
```

To generate random numbers of varied length, use the random function from NumPy.

```
np.random.rand(2,3)
> array([[ 0.41453991, 0.46230172, 0.78318915],
[0.54716578, 0.84263735, 0.60796399]])
```

Note   The random number seed can be set via numpy.random.
seed (1234). NumPy uses the Mersenne Twister algorithm to
generate pseudorandom numbers.

Pandas

Pandas is an open sourced software library. DataFrames and Series are two of its major data structures that are widely used for data analysis purposes. Series is a one-dimensional indexed array, and DataFrame is tabular data structure with column- and row-level indexes. Pandas is a great tool for preprocessing datasets and offers highly optimized performance.

```
import pandas as pd
series_1 = pd.Series([2,9,0,1])      # Creating a series object
print(series_1.values)               # Print values of the
                                            series object

> [2 9 0 1]

series_1.index             # Default index of the series object
> RangeIndex(start=0, stop=4, step=1)

series_1.index = ['a','b','c','d']   #Settnig index of the
                                            series object

series_1['d']                  # Fetching element using new index
> 1
```

```
# Creating dataframe using pandas
class_data = {'Names':['John','Ryan','Emily'],
              'Standard': [7,5,8],
              'Subject': ['English','Mathematics','Science']}
class_df = pd.DataFrame(class_data, index = ['Student1',
'Student2','Student3'],
                        columns = ['Names','Standard','Subject'])
print(class_df)
>           Names      Standard      Subject
Student1    John       7             English
Student2    Ryan       5             Mathematics
Student3    Emily      8             Science

class_df.Names
>Student1    John
Student2     Ryan
Student3     Emily
Name: Names, dtype: object

# Add new entry to the dataframe
import numpy as np
class_df.ix['Student4'] = ['Robin', np.nan, 'History']
class_df.T                      # Take transpose of the dataframe
>           Student1     Student2        Student3     Student4
Names       John         Ryan            Emily        Robin
Standard    7            5               8            NaN
Subject     English      Mathematics     Science      History
```

```
class_df.sort_values(by='Standard')    # Sorting of rows by one
                                         column
>           Names       Standard      Subject
Student1    John        7.0           English
Student2    Ryan        5.0           Mathematics
Student3    Emily       8.0           Science
Student4    Robin       NaN           History

# Adding one more column to the dataframe as Series object
col_entry = pd.Series(['A','B','A+','C'],
                      index=['Student1','Student2','Student3',
                      'Student4'])
class_df['Grade'] = col_entry
print(class_df)
>           Names       Standard      Subject        Grade
Student1    John        7.0           English        A
Student2    Ryan        5.0           Mathematics    B
Student3    Emily       8.0           Science        A+
Student4    Robin       NaN           History        C

# Filling the missing entries in the dataframe, inplace
class_df.fillna(10, inplace=True)
print(class_df)
>           Names       Standard      Subject        Grade
Student1    John        7.0           English        A
Student2    Ryan        5.0           Mathematics    B
Student3    Emily       8.0           Science        A+
Student4    Robin       10.0          History        C
```

```
# Concatenation of 2 dataframes
student_age = pd.DataFrame(data = {'Age': [13,10,15,18]} ,
                           index=['Student1','Student2',
                           'Student3','Student4'])
print(student_age)
>               Age
Student1        13
Student2        10
Student3        15
Student4        18

class_data = pd.concat([class_df, student_age], axis = 1)
print(class_data)
>          Names   Standard   Subject       Grade   Age
Student1   John    7.0        English       A       13
Student2   Ryan    5.0        Mathematics   B       10
Student3   Emily   8.0        Science       A+      15
Student4   Robin   10.0       History       C       18
```

Note   Use the map function to implement any function on each of the elements in a column/row individually and the apply function to perform any function on all the elements of a column/row simultaneously.

```
# MAP Function
class_data['Subject'] = class_data['Subject'].map(lambda x :
x + 'Sub')
class_data['Subject']
```

```
> Student1          EnglishSub
Student2          MathematicsSub
Student3          ScienceSub
Student4          HistorySub
Name: Subject, dtype: object

# APPLY Function
def age_add(x):                     # Defining a new function which
                                       will increment the age by 1

    return(x+1)

print('-----Old values-----')
print(class_data['Age'])
print('-----New values-----')
print(class_data['Age'].apply(age_add))     # Applying the age
                                               function on top of
                                               the age column

> -----Old values-----
Student1 13
Student2 10
Student3 15
Student4 18
Name: Age, dtype: int64

-----New values-----
Student1 14
Student2 11
Student3 16
Student4 19
Name: Age, dtype: int64
```

The following code is used to change the Datatype of the column to a "category" type:

```
# Changing datatype of the column
class_data['Grade'] = class_data['Grade'].astype('category')
class_data.Grade.dtypes
> category
```

The following stores the results to a .csv file:

```
# Storing the results
class_data.to_csv('class_dataset.csv', index=False)
```

Among the pool of functions offered by the Pandas library, merge functions (concat, merge, append), groupby, and pivot_table functions have an intensive application in data processing tasks. Refer to the following source for detailed Pandas tutorials: http://pandas.pydata.org/.

SciPy

SciPy offers complex algorithms and their use as functions in NumPy. This allocates high-level commands and a variety of classes to manipulate and visualize data. SciPy is curated in the form of multiple small packages, with each package targeting individual scientific computing domains. A few of the subpackages are linalg (linear algebra), constants (physical and mathematical constants), and sparse (sparse matrices and associated routines).

Most of the NumPy package functions applicable on arrays are also included in the SciPy package. SciPy offers pre-tested routines, thereby saving a lot of processing time in the scientific computing applications.

```
import scipy
import numpy as np
```

Note   SciPy offers in-built constructors for objects representing random variables.

Following are a few examples from Linalg and Stats out of multiple subpackages offered by SciPy. As the subpackages are domain-specific, it makes SciPy the perfect choice for data science.

SciPy subpackages, here for linear algebra (`scipy.linalg`), are supposed to be imported explicitly in the following manner:

```
from scipy import linalg
mat_ = np.array([[2,3,1], [4,9,10], [10,5,6]]) # Matrix Creation
print(mat_)
> [[ 2 3 1] [ 4 9 10] [10 5 6]]
```

```
linalg.det(mat_)                    # Determinant of the matrix
inv_mat = linalg.inv(mat_)          # Inverse of the matrix
print(inv_mat)
> [[ 0.02409639 -0.07831325 0.12650602] [ 0.45783133 0.01204819
-0.09638554] [-0.42168675 0.12048193 0.03614458]]
```

The code for performing singular value decomposition and storing the individual components follows:

```
# Singular Value Decomposition
comp_1, comp_2, comp_3 = linalg.svd(mat_)
print(comp_1)
print(comp_2)
print(comp_3)
```

```
> [[-0.1854159 0.0294175 -0.98221971]
 [-0.73602677 -0.66641413 0.11898237]
 [-0.65106493 0.74500122 0.14521585]]
 [ 18.34661713 5.73710697 1.57709968]
 [[-0.53555313 -0.56881403 -0.62420625]
 [ 0.84418693 -0.38076134 -0.37731848]
 [-0.02304957 -0.72902085 0.6841033 ]]
```

Scipy.stats is a huge subpackage, with various statistical distributions and functions for operations on different kinds of datasets.

```
# Scipy Stats module
from scipy import stats

# Generating a random sample of size 20 from normal
distribution with mean 3 and standard deviation 5
rvs_20 = stats.norm.rvs(3,5 , size = 20)
print(rvs_20, '\n --- ')

# Computing the CDF of Beta distribution with a=100 and b=130
as shape parameters at random variable 0.41
cdf_ = scipy.stats.beta.cdf(0.41, a=100, b=130)
print(cdf_)
> [ -0.21654555 7.99621694 -0.89264767 10.89089263 2.63297827
    -1.43167281 5.09490009 -2.0530585 -5.0128728 -0.54128795
     2.76283347 8.30919378 4.67849196 -0.74481568 8.28278981
    -3.57801485 -3.24949898 4.73948566 2.71580005 6.50054556]
---

0.225009574362
```

For in-depth examples using SciPy subpackages, refer to `http://docs.scipy.org/doc/`.

Introduction to Natural Language Processing

We already have seen the three most useful and frequently used libraries in Python. The examples and references provided should suffice to start with. Now, we are shifting our area of focus to natural language processing.

What Is Natural Language Processing?

Natural language processing, in its simplest form, is the ability for a computer/system to truly understand human language and process it in the same way that a human does.

Good Enough, But What Is the Big Deal?

It is very easy for humans to understand the language said/expressed by other humans. For example, if I say "America follows a capitalist form of economy, which works well for it, it is easy to infer that the *which* used in this sentence is associated with "capitalist form of economy," but how a computer/system will understand this is the question.

What Makes Natural Language Processing Difficult?

In a normal conversation between humans, things are often unsaid, whether in the form of some signal, expression, or just silence. Nevertheless, we, as humans, have the capacity to understand the underlying intent of the conversation, which a computer lacks.

A second difficulty is owing to ambiguity in sentences. This may be at the word level, at the sentence level, or at the meaning level.

Ambiguity at Word Level

Consider the word *won't*. There is always an ambiguity associated with the word. Will the system treat the contraction as one word or two words, and in what sense (what will its meaning be?).

Ambiguity at Sentence Level

Consider the following sentences:

Most of the time travelers worry about their luggage.

Without punctuation, it is hard to infer from the given sentence whether "time travelers" worry about their luggage or merely "travelers."

Time flies like an arrow.

The rate at which time is spent is compared to the speed of an arrow, which is quite difficult to map, given only this sentence and without enough information concerning the general nature of the two entities mentioned.

Ambiguity at Meaning Level

Consider the word *tie*. There are three ways in which you can process (interpret) this word: as an equal score between contestants, as a garment, and as a verb.

Figure 1-1 illustrates a simple Google Translate failure. It assumes fan to mean an admirer and not an object.

Figure 1-1. *Example of Google Translate from English to Hindi*

These are just few of the endless challenges you will encounter while working in NLP. As we proceed further, we will explore how to deal with them.

What Do We Want to Achieve Through Natural Language Processing?

There is no limit to what can be achieved through NLP. There are, however, some common applications of NLP, principally the following:

- Text Summarization

Remember your school days, when the teacher used to ask the class to summarize a block of text? This task could well have been achieved using NLP.

- Text Tagging

NLP can be used effectively to find the context of a whole bunch of text (topic tagging).

- Named Entity Recognition

This can determine whether a word or word-group represents a place, organization, or anything else.

- Chatbot

The most talked-about application of NLP is Chatbot. It can find the intent of the question asked by a user and send an appropriate reply, achieved through the training process.

- Speech Recognition

This application recognizes a spoken language and transforms it into text.

As discussed, there are numerous applications for NLP. The idea is not to get intimidated by them but to learn and develop one or more such applications by yourself.

Common Terms Associated with Language Processing

As we move further and further along, there are a few terms that you will encounter frequently. Therefore, it is a good idea to become acquainted with them as soon as possible.

- Phonetics/phonology

The study of linguistic sounds and their relations to written words

- Morphology

The study of internal structures of words/composition of words

- Syntax

The study of the structural relationships among words in a sentence

- Semantics

The study of the meaning of words and how these combine to form the meaning of sentences

- Pragmatics

Situational use of language sentences

- Discourse

A linguistic unit that is larger than a single sentence (context)

Natural Language Processing Libraries

Following are basic examples from some of the most frequently used NLP libraries in Python.

NLTK

NLTK (www.nltk.org/) is the most common package you will encounter working with corpora, categorizing text, analyzing linguistic structure, and more.

Note   Following is the recommended way of installing the NLTK package: `pip install nltk`.

You can tokenize a given sentence into individual words, as follows:

```
import nltk
# Tokenization
sent_ = "I am almost dead this time"
tokens_ = nltk.word_tokenize(sent_)
tokens_
>> ['I', 'am', 'almost', 'dead', 'this', 'time']
```

Getting a synonym of a word. One can get lists of synonyms for a word using NLTK.

```
# Make sure to install wordnet, if not done already so
# import nltk
# nltk.download('wordnet')
# Synonyms
from nltk.corpus import wordnet
word_ = wordnet.synsets("spectacular")
print(word_)
>> [Synset('spectacular.n.01'), Synset('dramatic.s.02'),
Synset('spectacular.s.02'), Synset('outstanding.s.02')]
print(word_[0].definition())      # Printing the meaning along
                                      of each of the synonyms
print(word_[1].definition())
print(word_[2].definition())
print(word_[3].definition())
>> a lavishly produced performance
>> sensational in appearance or thrilling in effect
>> characteristic of spectacles or drama
>> having a quality that thrusts itself into attention
```

Stemming and lemmatizing words. Word *Stemming* means removing affixes from words and returning the root word (which may not be a real word). Lemmatizing is similar to stemming, but the difference is that the result of lemmatizing is a real word.

```
# Stemming
from nltk.stem import PorterStemmer
stemmer = PorterStemmer()              # Create the stemmer object
```

```
print(stemmer.stem("decreases"))
>> decreas

#Lemmatization
from nltk.stem import WordNetLemmatizer
lemmatizer = WordNetLemmatizer()      # Create the Lemmatizer
                                           object
print(lemmatizer.lemmatize("decreases"))
>> decrease
```

TextBlob

TextBlob (http://textblob.readthedocs.io/en/dev/index.html) is a Python library for processing textual data. It provides a simple API for diving deep into common NLP tasks, such as part-of-speech tagging, noun phrase extraction, sentiment analysis, classification, and much more. You can use it for sentiment analysis. Sentiment refers to a feeling hidden in the sentence. Polarity defines negativity or positivity in the sentence, whereas subjectivity implies whether the sentence discusses something vaguely or with complete surety.

```
from textblob import TextBlob
# Taking a statement as input
statement = TextBlob("My home is far away from my school.")
# Calculating the sentiment attached with the statement
statement.sentiment
Sentiment(polarity=0.1, subjectivity=1.0)
```

You can also use TextBlob for tagging purposes. Tagging is the process of denoting a word in a text (corpus) as corresponding to a particular part of speech.

```
# Defining a sample text
text = '''How about you and I go together on a walk far away
from this place, discussing the things we have never discussed
on Deep Learning and Natural Language Processing.'''
blob_ = TextBlob(text)          # Making it as Textblob object
blob_
>> TextBlob("How about you and I go together on a walk far away
from this place, discussing the things we have never discussed
on Deep Learning and Natural Language Processing.")
# This part internally makes use of the 'punkt' resource from
   the NLTK package, make sure to download it before running this
# import nltk
# nltk.download('punkt')
# nltk.download('averaged_perceptron_tagger')
# Running this separately : python3.6 -m textblob.download_
   corpora
blob_.tags
>>
[('How', 'WRB'),
 ('about', 'IN'),
 ('you', 'PRP'),
 ('and', 'CC'),
 ('I', 'PRP'),
 ('go', 'VBP'),
 ('together', 'RB'),
 ('on', 'IN'),
 ('a', 'DT'),
 ('walk', 'NN'),
 ('far', 'RB'),
 ('away', 'RB'),
```

```
('from', 'IN'),
('this', 'DT'),
('place', 'NN'),
('discussing', 'VBG'),
('the', 'DT'),
('things', 'NNS'),
('we', 'PRP'),
('have', 'VBP'),
('never', 'RB'),
('discussed', 'VBN'),
('on', 'IN'),
('Deep', 'NNP'),
('Learning', 'NNP'),
('and', 'CC'),
('Natural', 'NNP'),
('Language', 'NNP'),
('Processing', 'NNP')]
```

You can use TextBlob to deal with spelling errors.

```
sample_ = TextBlob("I thinkk the model needs to be trained more!")
print(sample_.correct())
>> I think the model needs to be trained more!
```

Furthermore, the package offers language a translation module.

```
# Language Translation
lang_ = TextBlob(u"Voulez-vous apprendre le français?")
lang_.translate(from_lang='fr', to='en')
>> TextBlob("Do you want to learn French?")
```

SpaCy

SpaCy (`https://spacy.io/`) provides very fast and accurate syntactic analysis (the fastest of any library released) and also offers named entity recognition and ready access to word vectors. It is written in Cython language and contains a wide variety of trained models on language vocabularies, syntaxes, word-to-vector transformations, and entities recognition.

Note   *Entity recognition* is the process used to classify multiple entities found in a text in predefined categories, such as a person, objects, location, organizations, dates, events, etc. *Word vector* refers to the mapping of the words or phrases from vocabulary to a vector of real numbers.

```
import spacy
# Run below command, if you are getting error
# python -m spacy download en
nlp = spacy.load("en")

william_wikidef = """William was the son of King William
II and Anna Pavlovna of Russia. On the abdication of his
grandfather  William I in 1840, he became the Prince of Orange.
On the death of his father in 1849, he succeeded as king of the
Netherlands. William married his cousin Sophie of Württemberg
in 1839 and they had three sons, William, Maurice, and
Alexander, all of whom predeceased him. """

nlp_william = nlp(william_wikidef)

print([ (i, i.label_, i.label) for i in nlp_william.ents])
```

```
>> [(William, 'PERSON', 378), (William II, 'PERSON', 378),
(Anna Pavlovna, 'PERSON', 378), (Russia, 'GPE', 382), (
, 'GPE', 382), (William, 'PERSON', 378), (1840, 'DATE', 388),
(the Prince of Orange, 'LOC', 383), (1849, 'DATE', 388),
(Netherlands, 'GPE', 382), (
, 'GPE', 382), (William, 'PERSON', 378), (Sophie, 'GPE', 382),
(Württemberg, 'PERSON', 378), (1839, 'DATE', 388), (three,
'CARDINAL', 394), (William, 'PERSON', 378), (Maurice, 'PERSON',
378), (Alexander, 'GPE', 382), (
, 'GPE', 382)]
```

SpaCy also offers dependency parsing, which could be further utilized to extract noun phrases from the text, as follows:

```
# Noun Phrase extraction
senten_ = nlp('The book deals with NLP')
for noun_ in senten_.noun_chunks:
    print(noun_)
    print(noun_.text)
    print('---')
    print(noun_.root.dep_)
    print('---')
    print(noun_.root.head.text)
>> The book
The book
---
nsubj
---
deals
NLP
NLP
---
```

```
pobj
---
with
```

Gensim

Gensim (`https://pypi.python.org/pypi/gensim`) is another important library. It is used primarily for topic modeling and document similarity. Gensim is most useful for tasks such as getting a word vector of a word.

```
from gensim.models import Word2Vec
min_count = 0
size = 50
window = 2
sentences= "bitcoin is an innovative payment network and a new
kind of money."
sentences=sentences.split()
print(sentences)
>> ['bitcoin', 'is', 'an', 'innovative', 'payment', 'network',
'and', 'a', 'new', 'kind', 'of', 'money.']
model = Word2Vec(sentences, min_count=min_count, size=size,
window=window)
model
>> <gensim.models.word2vec.Word2Vec at 0x7fd1d889e710>
model['a']            # Vector for the character 'a'
>> array([  9.70041566e-03,  -4.16209083e-03,   8.05089157e-03,
          4.81479801e-03,   1.93488982e-03,  -4.19071550e-03,
          1.41675305e-03,  -6.54719025e-03,   3.92444432e-03,
         -7.05081783e-03,   7.69438222e-03,   3.89579940e-03,
         -9.02676862e-03,  -8.58401007e-04,  -3.24096601e-03,
          9.24982232e-05,   7.13059027e-03,   8.80233292e-03,
         -2.46750680e-03,  -5.17094415e-03,   2.74592242e-03,
```

```
         4.08304436e-03,   -7.59716751e-03,    8.94313212e-03,
        -8.39354657e-03,    5.89343486e-03,    3.76902265e-03,
         8.84669367e-04,    1.63217512e-04,    8.95449053e-03,
        -3.24510527e-03,    3.52341868e-03,    6.98625855e-03,
        -5.50296041e-04,   -5.10712992e-03,   -8.52414686e-03,
        -3.00202984e-03,   -5.32727176e-03,   -8.02035537e-03,
        -9.11156740e-03,   -7.68519414e-04,   -8.95629171e-03,
        -1.65163784e-03,    9.59598401e-04,    9.03090648e-03,
         5.31166652e-03,    5.59739536e-03,   -4.49402537e-03,
        -6.75261812e-03,   -5.75679634e-03], dtype=float32)
```

One can download the trained set of vectors from Google and figure out the representation for desired text, as follows:

```
model = gensim.models.KeyedVectors.load_word2vec_
format('GoogleNews-vectors-negative300.bin', binary=True)
sentence = ["I", "hope", "it", "is", "going", "good", "for", "you"]
vectors = [model[w] for w in sentence]
```

(You can use the following link to download the sample model: https://github.com/mmihaltz/word2vec-GoogleNews-vectors, or undertake a conventional search with the given name of the .bin file and paste it in your working directory.)

Gensim offers LDA (latent dirichlet allocation—a generative statistical model that allows sets of observations to be explained by unobserved groups that explain why some parts of the data are similar) modules too. This allows both LDA model estimation from a training corpus and inference of topic distribution on new, unseen documents. The model can also be updated with new documents for online training.

Pattern

Pattern (`https://pypi.python.org/pypi/Pattern`) is useful for a variety of NLP tasks, such as part-of-speech taggers, n-gram searches, sentiment analysis, and WordNet and machine learning, such as vector space modeling, k-means clustering, Naive Bayes, K-NN, and SVM classifiers.

```
import pattern
from pattern.en import tag
tweet_ = "I hope it is going good for you!"
tweet_l = tweet_.lower()
tweet_tags = tag(tweet_l)
print(tweet_tags)
>> [('i', 'JJ'), ('hope', 'NN'), ('it', 'PRP'), ('is', 'VBZ'),
('going', 'VBG'), ('good', 'JJ'), ('for', 'IN'), ('you',
'PRP'), ('!', '.')]
```

Stanford CoreNLP

Stanford CoreNLP (`https://stanfordnlp.github.io/CoreNLP/`) provides the base forms of words; their parts of speech; whether they are names of companies, people, etc.; normalizes dates, times, and numeric quantities; marks up the structure of sentences in terms of phrases and syntactic dependencies; indicates which noun phrases refer to the same entities; indicates sentiment; extracts particular or open-class relations between entity mentions; gets the quotes people said; etc.

Getting Started with NLP

In this part of the chapter, we are going to take a simple text data (such as a sentence) and perform some basic operations to get acquainted with how NLP works. This part will provide a foundation for what you are going to learn in the rest of the book.

Text Search Using Regular Expressions

Regular expressions are a very useful means of searching for a particular type of design or wordset from a given text. A regular expression (RE) specifies a set of strings that match it. The functions in this module allow you to check if a given string matches a particular RE (or if a given RE matches a particular string, which comes down to the same thing).

```
# Text search across the sentence using Regular expression
import re
words = ['very','nice','lecture','day','moon']
expression = '|'.join(words)
re.findall(expression, 'i attended a very nice lecture last
year', re.M)
>> ['very', 'nice', 'lecture']
```

Text to List

You can read a text file and convert it into a list of words or list of sentences, according to your needs.

```
text_file = 'data.txt'
# Method-1 : Individual words as separate elements of the list
with open(text_file) as f:
    words = f.read().split()
print(words)
>> ['Are', 'you', 'sure', 'moving', 'ahead', 'on', 'this',
'route', 'is', 'the', 'right', 'thing?']

# Method-2 : Whole text as single element of the list
f = open(text_file , 'r')
words_ = f.readlines()
```

```
print(words_)
>> ['Are you sure moving ahead on this route is the right
thing?\n']
```

Preprocessing the Text

There is a large number of things you could do to preprocess the text. For example, replacing one word with another, removing or adding some specific type of words, etc.

```
sentence = 'John has been selected for the trial phase this
time. Congrats!!'
sentence=sentence.lower()
# defining the positive and negative words explicitly
positive_words=['awesome','good', 'nice', 'super', 'fun',
'delightful','congrats']
negative_words=['awful','lame','horrible','bad']
sentence=sentence.replace('!','')
sentence
>> 'john has been selected for the trial phase this time.
congrats'
words= sentence.split(' ')
print(words)
>> ['john', 'has', 'been', 'selected', 'for', 'the', 'trial',
'phase', 'this', 'time.', 'congrats']
result= set(words)-set(positive_words)
print(result)
>> {'has', 'phase', 'for', 'time.', 'trial', 'been', 'john',
'the', 'this', 'selected'}
```

Accessing Text from the Web

A text file from a URL can be accessed using urllib.

```
# Make sure both the packages are installed
import urllib3
from bs4 import BeautifulSoup
pool_object = urllib3.PoolManager()
target_url = 'http://www.gutenberg.org/files/2554/2554-
h/2554-h.htm#link2HCH0008'
response_ = pool_object.request('GET', target_url)
final_html_txt = BeautifulSoup(response_.data)
print(final_html_txt)
```

Removal of Stopwords

A stopword is a commonly used word (such as *the*) that a search engine has been programmed to ignore.

```
import nltk
from nltk import word_tokenize
sentence= "This book is about Deep Learning and Natural
Language Processing!"
tokens = word_tokenize(sentence)
print(tokens)
>> ['This', 'book', 'is', 'about', 'Deep', 'Learning', 'and',
'Natural', 'Language', 'Processing', '!']
# nltk.download('stopwords')
from nltk.corpus import stopwords
stop_words = set(stopwords.words('english'))
new_tokens = [w for w in tokens if not w in stop_words]
new_tokens
>> ['This', 'book', 'Deep', 'Learning', 'Natural', 'Language',
'Processing', '!']
```

Counter Vectorization

Counter vectorization is a SciKit-Learn library tool that takes any mass of text and returns each unique word as a feature, with a count of the number of times a particular word occurs in the text.

```
from sklearn.feature_extraction.text import CountVectorizer
texts=["Ramiess sings classic songs","he listens to old pop ",
"and rock music", ' and also listens to classical songs']
cv = CountVectorizer()
cv_fit=cv.fit_transform(texts)
print(cv.get_feature_names())
print(cv_fit.toarray())
>> ['also', 'and', 'classic', 'classical', 'he', 'listens',
'listens', 'music', 'old', 'pop', 'ramiess', 'rock', 'sings',
'songs', 'to']
>> [[0 0 1 0 0 0 0 0 0 0 1 0 1 1 0]
    [0 0 0 0 1 1 0 0 1 1 0 0 0 0 1]
    [0 1 0 0 0 0 0 1 0 0 0 1 0 0 0]
    [1 1 0 1 0 0 1 0 0 0 0 0 0 1 0]]
```

TF-IDF Score

TF-IDF is an acronym of two terms: term frequency and inverse document frequency. TF is the ratio representing the count of specific words to the total number of words in a document. Suppose that a document contains 100 words, wherein the word *happy* appears five times. The term frequency (i.e., tf) for *happy* is then $(5/100) = 0.05$. IDF, on the other hand, is a log ratio of the total number of documents to a document containing a particular word. Suppose we have 10 million documents, and the word *happy* appears in 1,000 of them. The inverse document frequency (i.e., idf), then, would be calculated as $\log(10,000,000/1,000) = 4$. Thus, the TF-IDF weight is the product of these quantities: $0.05 \times 4 = 0.20$.

> **Note**   Along similar lines as TF-IDF is BM25, which is used to score a document on the basis of its relation to a query. BM25 ranks a set of documents using the query terms of each of the documents, irrespective of the relationship between the keywords of the query within a document.

```
from sklearn.feature_extraction.text import TfidfVectorizer
texts=["Ramiess sings classic songs","he listens to old pop",
"and rock music", ' and also listens to classical songs']
vect = TfidfVectorizer()
X = vect.fit_transform(texts)
print(X.todense())
>> [[ 0.           0.           0.52547275  0.           0.
       0.           0.
   0.           0.           0.          0.52547275  0.
       0.52547275
   0.41428875   0.           ]
 [ 0.           0.           0.          0.          0.4472136
       0.4472136
   0.           0.          0.4472136   0.4472136   0.
       0.           0.
   0.           0.4472136 ]
 [ 0.          0.48693426   0.          0.          0.
       0.           0.
   0.61761437   0.          0.          0.          0.61761437
       0.           0.
   0.           ]
 [ 0.48546061   0.38274272   0.          0.48546061  0.
       0.
```

```
 0.48546061      0.            0.            0.            0.
         0.            0.
 0.38274272      0.            ]]
```

Text Classifier

Text can be classified into various classes, such as positive and negative. TextBlob offers many such architectures.

```
from textblob import TextBlob
from textblob.classifiers import NaiveBayesClassifier
data = [
 ('I love my country.', 'pos'),
 ('This is an amazing place!', 'pos'),
 ('I do not like the smell of this place.', 'neg'),
 ('I do not like this restaurant', 'neg'),
 ('I am tired of hearing your nonsense.', 'neg'),
 ("I always aspire to be like him", 'pos'),
 ("It's a horrible performance.", "neg")
 ]
model = NaiveBayesClassifier(data)
model.classify("It's an awesome place!")
>> 'pos'
```

Introduction to Deep Learning

Deep learning is an extended field of machine learning that has proven to be highly useful in the domains of text, image, and speech, primarily. The collection of algorithms implemented under deep learning have similarities with the relationship between stimuli and neurons in the human brain. Deep learning has extensive applications in computer vision, language translation, speech recognition, image generation, and so forth. These sets of algorithms are simple enough to learn in both a supervised and unsupervised fashion.

A majority of deep learning algorithms are based on the concept of artificial neural networks, and the training of such algorithms in today's world has been made easier with the availability of abundant data and sufficient computation resources. With additional data, the performance of deep learning models just keep on improving. A better representation of this can be seen in Figure 1-2.

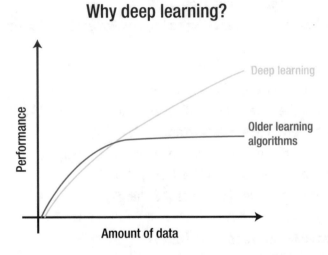

Figure 1-2. *Scaling data science techniques to amount of data*

The term *deep* in deep learning refers to the depth of the artificial neural network architecture, and *learning* stands for learning through the artificial neural network itself. Figure 1-3 is an accurate representation of the difference between a deep and a shallow network and why the term *deep learning* gained currency.

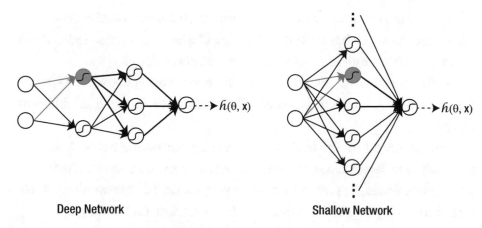

Figure 1-3. *Representation of deep and shallow networks*

Deep neural networks are capable of discovering latent structures (or feature learning) from unlabeled and unstructured data, such as images (pixel data), documents (text data), or files (audio, video data).

Although an artificial neural network and models in deep learning fundamentally hold similar structures, this does not translate to mean that a combination of two artificial neural networks will perform similarly to a deep neural network when trained to use the data.

What differentiates any deep neural network from an ordinary artificial neural network is the way we use backpropagation. In an ordinary artificial neural network, backpropagation trains later (or end) layers more efficiently than it trains initial (or former) layers. Thus, as we travel back into the network, errors become smaller and more diffused.

How Deep Is "Deep"?

We hear the term *deep* and instantly become intimated by it, but there is not much difference between a shallow and deep neural network. A deep neural network is simply a feed forward neural network with multiple hidden layers. Yes, it's that simple!

If there are many layers in the network, then we say that the network is deep. The question that should be flashing through your mind right now is how many layers must a network have to qualify as deep?

Before we start our actual journey on deep learning in the NLP space, it would be useful to review the basics of neural networks and their different types.

We will introduce the basic structure of a basic neural network and a few of the different types of the neural networks used across industry-wide applications. To provide a concise yet practical understanding of this technique, this part of the chapter is subdivided into six headings:

- What Are Neural Networks?

- Basic Structure of Neural Networks

- Types of Neural Networks

- Multilayer Perceptrons

- Stochastic Gradient Descent

- Backpropagation

Note   For a detailed academic understanding, you can refer to treatises and articles published by Geoffrey Hinton (`www.cs.toronto.edu/~hinton/`) and others (`http://deeplearning.net/`).

What Are Neural Networks?

Neural networks have a long history that can be traced back to the seminal works of Marvin Minsky on artificial intelligence (AI) and his (in)famous reference to the challenge of solving an exclusive OR (XOR) function. Neural networks have become increasingly prevalent, as major advances have been made, with access to larger and larger datasets and the advent of cloud computing and GPUs that provide immense computing power. This ready access to data and computing has produced better accuracy in modeling and analytics.

Neural networks are a biologically inspired paradigm (imitating the functioning of the mammalian brain) that enables a computer to learn human faculties from observational data. They currently provide solutions to many problems: image recognition, handwriting recognition, speech recognition, speech analysis, and NLP.

To help us develop an intuitive sense, the different tasks we perform during a day can be categorized as follows:

> algebraic or linear inference (e.g., $A \times B = C$, or a series of tasks, such as a recipe for a cake)
>
> recognition perception or nonlinear inference (e.g., associating names with photos of animals or reducing stress or validating a statement based on voice analysis)
>
> learning a task through observation (e.g., navigation in the Google car)

The first task can be addressed algorithmically, i.e., described programmatically to produce a result from numbers or ingredients, whereas it's difficult, if not impossible, to define an algorithmic approach for the latter tasks. The latter tasks require a flexible model that can autonomously adapt its behavior, based on tagged examples.

Now, statistical or optimization algorithms also strive to provide correct output[s] in relation to possible input[s], though they require the specification of a function to model the data for which they produce the optimal set of coefficients. In contrast to optimization techniques, a neural network is a flexible function that autonomously adapts its behavior to satisfy as much as possible the relation between the input[s] and the expected result[s] and has been termed as a universal approximator.

Given the pervasive use of algorithms, there are libraries (Figure 1-4) available on all popular platforms, such as R (knn, nnet packages), Scala (machine learning ML extensions), and Python (TensorFlow, MXNet, Keras).

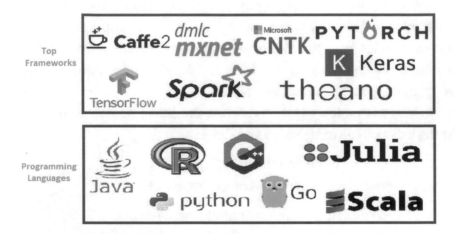

Figure 1-4. *Multiple open source platforms and libraries for deep learning*

Basic Structure of Neural Networks

The basic principle behind a neural network is a collection of basic elements, *artificial neuron* or *perceptron*, that were first developed in the 1950s by Frank Rosenblatt. They take several binary inputs, $x_1, x_2, ..., x_N$ and produce a single binary output if the sum is greater than the *activation potential*. The neuron is said to "fire" whenever activation potential is exceeded and behaves as a step function. The neurons that fire pass along the signal to other neurons connected to their dendrites, which, in turn, will fire, if the activation potential is exceeded, thus producing a cascading effect (Figure 1-5).

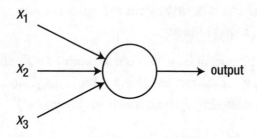

Figure 1-5. *Sample neuron*

As not all inputs have the same emphasis, weights are attached to each of the inputs, x_i to allow the model to assign more importance to some inputs. Thus, output is 1, if the weighted sum is greater than activation potential or bias, i.e.,

$$\text{Output} = \Sigma_j w_j x_j + Bias$$

In practice, this simple form is difficult, owing to the abrupt nature of the step function (Figure 1-6). So, a modified form was created to behave more predictably, i.e., small changes in weights and bias cause only a small change in output. There are two main modifications.

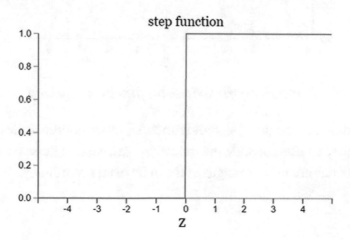

Figure 1-6. *Step function*

1. The inputs can take on any value between 0 and 1, instead of being binary.

2. To make the output behave more smoothly for given inputs, $x_1, x_2, ..., x_N$, and weights. $w_1, w_2, ..., w_N$, and bias, b, use the following sigmoid function (Figure 1-7):

$$1/\left(1+\exp\left(-\sum_j w_j x_j - b\right)\right)$$

The smoothness of the exponential function, or σ, means that small changes in weights and bias will produce a small change in the output from the neuron (the change could be a linear function of changes in weights and bias).

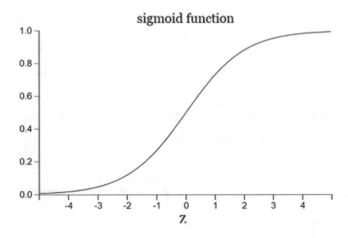

Figure 1-7. *Neural network activation function: sigmoid*

In addition to the usual sigmoid function, other nonlinearities that are more frequently used include the following, and each of these could have similar or different output ranges and can be used accordingly.

- **ReLU**: Rectified linear unit. This keeps the activation guarded at zero. It is computed using the following function:

$$Z_j = f_j\left(x_j\right) = \max\left(0, x_j\right)$$

where, x_j, the j-th input value, and z_j is its corresponding output value after the ReLU function f. Following is the graph (Figure 1-8) of the ReLU function, with '0' value for all $x <= 0$, and with a linear slope of 1 for all $x > 0$:

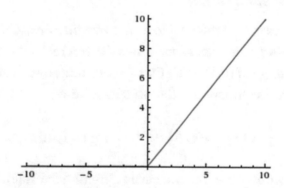

***Figure 1-8.** ReLU function graph*

ReLUs quite often face the issue of dying, especially when the learning rate is set to a higher value, as this triggers weight updating that doesn't allow the activation of the specific neurons, thereby making the gradient of that neuron forever zero. Another risk offered by ReLU is the explosion of the activation function, as the input value, x_j, is itself the output here. Although ReLU offers other benefits as well, such as the introduction of sparsity in cases where x_j is below 0, leading to sparse representations, and as the gradient returned in cases where ReLU is constant, it results in faster learning, accompanied by the reduced likelihood of the gradient vanishing.

- **LReLUs (Leaky ReLUs)**: These mitigate the issue of dying ReLUs by introducing a marginally reduced slope (~0.01) for values of x less than 0. LReLUs do offer successful scenarios, although not always.

- **ELU (Exponential Linear Unit)**: These offer negative values that push the mean unit activations closer to zero, thereby speeding the learning process, by moving the nearby gradient to the unit natural gradient. For a better explanation of ELUs, refer to the original paper by Djork-Arné Clevert, available at `https://arxiv.org/abs/1511.07289`.

- **Softmax**: Also referred to as a *normalized exponential function*, this transforms a set of given real values in the range of (0,1), such that the combined sum is 1. A softmax function is denoted as follows:

$$\sigma\left(z\right)_j = e^{z_k} / \sum_{k=1}^{k} e^{z_k} \qquad \text{for } j = 1, \ldots, K$$

All the preceding functions are easily differentiable, allowing the network to be trained easily with gradient descent (covered in the next section, "Types of Neural Networks").

As in the mammalian brain, individual neurons are organized in *layers*, with *connections* within a layer and to the next layer, creating an ANN, or artificial neural network or multilayer perceptron (MLP). As you may have guessed, the complexity is based on the number of elements and the number of neighbors connected.

The layers between input and output are referred to as *hidden layers*, and the density and type of connections between layers is the *configuration*. For example, a fully connected configuration has all the neurons of layer L connected to those of $L + 1$. For a more pronounced localization, we can connect only a local neighborhood, say nine neurons, to the next layer. Figure 1-9 illustrates two hidden layers with dense connections.

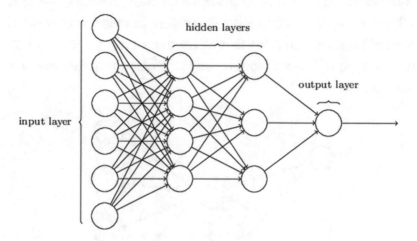

Figure 1-9. *Neural network architecture*

Types of Neural Networks

Up until now, we've been discussing artificial neural networks in general; however, there are different types of neural networks, based on architecture and usage. For neural networks to learn in a faster and more efficient way, various neurons are placed in the network in such a way as to maximize the learning of the network for the given problem. This placing of neurons follows a sensible approach and results in an architectural network design with different neurons consuming the output of other neurons, or different functions taking output from other functions in their inputs. If the neurons are placed with connections among them taking the form of cycles, then they form networks such as feedback, recursive, or recurrent neural networks. If, however, the connections between the neurons are acyclic, they form networks such as feedforward neural networks. Following are detailed explanations of the networks cited.

Feedforward Neural Networks

Feedforward neural networks constitute the basic units of the neural network family. Data movement in any feedforward neural network is from the input layer to output layer, via present hidden layers, restricting any kind of loops (Figure 1-10). Output from one layer serves as input to the next layer, with restrictions on any kind of loops in the network architecture.

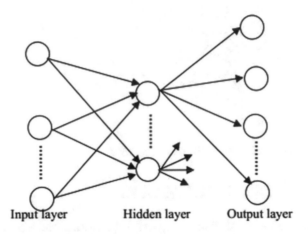

Figure 1-10. *A multilayer feedforward neural network*

Convolutional Neural Networks

Convolutional neural networks are well adapted for image recognition and handwriting recognition. Their structure is based on sampling a window or portion of an image, detecting its features, and then using the features to build a representation. As is evident by this description, this leads to the use of several layers, thus these models were the first deep learning models.

Recurrent Neural Networks

Recurrent neural networks (RNNs; Figure 1-11) are used when a data pattern changes over time. RNNs can be assumed as unrolled over time. An RNN applies the same layer to the input at each time step, using the output (i.e., the state of previous time steps as inputs).

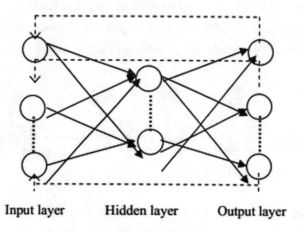

Input layer   Hidden layer   Output layer

Figure 1-11. *Recurrent neural network*

RNNs have feedback loops in which the output from the previous firing or time index T is fed as one of the inputs at time index T + 1. There might be cases in which the output of the neuron is fed to itself as input. As these are well-suited for applications involving sequences, they are widely used in problems related to videos, which are a time sequence of images, and for translation purposes, wherein understanding the next word is based on the context of the previous text. Following are various types of RNNs:

> **Encoding recurrent neural networks**: This set of RNNs enables the network to take an input of the sequence form (Figure 1-12).

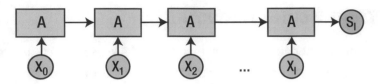

Figure 1-12. *Encoding RNNs*

Generating recurrent neural networks: Such networks basically output a sequence of numbers or values, like words in a sentence (Figure 1-13).

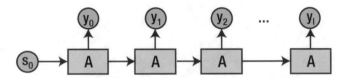

Figure 1-13. *Generating RNNs*

General recurrent neural networks: These networks are a combination of the preceding two types of RNNs. General RNNs (Figure 1-14) are used to generate sequences and, thus, are widely used in NLG (natural language generation) tasks.

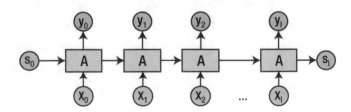

Figure 1-14. *General RNNs*

Encoder-Decoder Networks

Encoder-decoder networks use one network to create an internal representation of the input, or to "encode" it, and that representation is used as an input for another network to produce the output. This is useful to go beyond a classification of the input. The final output can be in the same modality, i.e., language translation, or a different modality, e.g., text tagging of an image, based on concepts. For reference, one can refer to the paper "Sequence to Sequence Learning with Neural Networks," published by the team at Google: (https://papers.nips.cc/paper/5346-sequence-to-sequence-learning-with-neural-networks.pdf).

Recursive Neural Networks

In a recursive neural network (Figure 1-15), a fixed set of weights is recursively applied onto the network structure and is primarily used to discover the hierarchy or structure of the data. Whereas an RNN is a chain, a recursive neural network takes the form of a treelike structure. Such networks have great use in the field of NLP, such as to decipher the sentiment of a sentence. The overall sentiment is not dependent on the individual works only, but also on the order in which the words are syntactically grouped in the sentence.

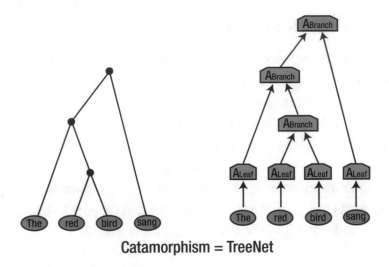

Catamorphism = TreeNet

Figure 1-15. *Recursive neural network*

As one can see, there are different types of networks, and while some can be applied in many different contexts, specific ones are better suited to certain applications, in terms of speed and quality.

Multilayer Perceptrons

Multilayer perceptrons (MLPs) belong to the category of feedforward neural networks and are made up of three types of layers: an input layer, one or more hidden layers, and a final output layer. A normal MLP has the following properties:

- Hidden layers with any number of neurons

- An input layer using linear functions

- Hidden layer(s) using an activation function, such as sigmoid

- An activation function giving any number of outputs

- Proper established connections between the input
  layer, hidden layer(s), and output layer

MLPs are also known as universal approximators, as they can find
the relationship between the input values and the targets, by using a
sufficient number of neurons in the hidden layer, altering weights, or by
using additional training data to approximate the given function up to
any level of accuracy. This doesn't even require a significant amount of
prior information about mapping between input and output values. Often,
with the given degree of freedom to an MLP, it can outperform the basic
MLP network, by introducing more hidden layers, with fewer neurons in
each of the hidden layers and optimum weights. This helps in the overall
generalization process of the model.

Following are a few of the features of network architecture that have a
direct impact on its performance

- **Hidden layers**: These contribute to the generalization
  factor of the network. In most cases, a single layer is
  sufficient to encompass the approximation of any desired
  function, supported with a sufficient number of neurons.

- **Hidden neurons**: The number of neurons present
  across the hidden layer(s) that can be selected by using
  any kind of formulation. A basic rule of thumb is to
  select count between one and a few input units. Another
  means is to use cross-validation and then check the
  plot between the number of neurons in the hidden
  layer(s) and the average mean squared error (MSE) with
  respect to each of the combinations, finally selecting the
  combination with the least MSE value. It also depends
  on the degree of nonlinearity or the initial problem
  dimensionality. It is, thus, more of an adaptive process
  to add/delete the neurons.

- **Output nodes**: The count of output nodes is usually equal to the number of classes we want to classify the target value.

- **Activation functions**: These are applied on the inputs of individual nodes. A set of nonlinear functions, described in detail in the *Basic Structure of Neural Networks* section of this chapter, are used to make the output fall within a desired range, thereby preventing the paralysis of the network. In addition to the nonlinearity, the continuous differentiability of these functions helps in preventing the inhibition of the training of neural networks.

As the output given by an MLP depends only on the current input and not on past or future inputs, so MLPs are considered apt for resolving classification problems.

Figure 1-16 shows that there are a total of $(L + 2)$ layers in the MLP, with the input layer at the first position, followed by L hidden layers and, finally, the output layer at the $(L + 2)$-th position. The following equations define the different units of the MLP, with activation functions applied at different stages of the network.

$W(k)$ denotes the weight connection between the k-th hidden layer and the layer before it, the input layer, or another hidden layer. Each $W(k)$ is made up of weights, $W_{ij}^{(k)}$, between the units i and j of the two connecting layers. $b(k)$ is the bias for the k-th layer.

The following equation represents the hidden layer preactivation for $k > 0$:

$$a^{(k)}(x) = b^{(k)} + W^{(k)} h^{(k-1)}(x)$$

For any i-th neuron present in the k-th hidden layer, the following equation holds true:

$$h^{(k)}(x)_i = g\left(a^{(k)}(x)_i\right)$$

The activation function for the output layer $(k = L + 1)$ follows:

$$h^{(L+1)}(x) = o\left(a^{(L+1)}(x)\right) = f(x)$$

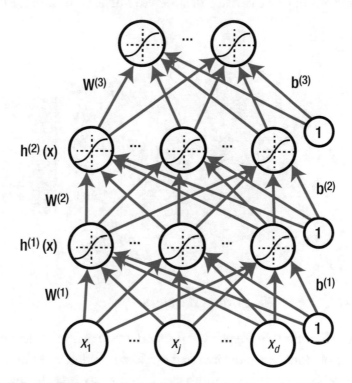

Figure 1-16. *Multilayer neural network*

Stochastic Gradient Descent

The workhorse of almost all solutions to optimization problems is the gradient descent algorithm. It is an iterative algorithm that minimizes a loss function by subsequently updating the parameters of the function.

As we can see from Figure 1-17, we start by thinking of our function as a kind of a valley. We imagine a ball rolling down the slope of a valley. Our everyday experience tells us that the ball will eventually roll to the bottom of the valley. Perhaps we can use this idea to find a minimum for the cost function.

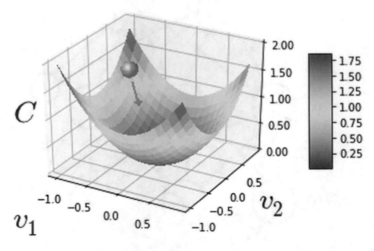

Figure 1-17. *Ball rolling down the slope*

Here the function we are using is dependent on two variables: *v1* and *v2*. This may be obvious, given the fact that our loss function looks like the one preceding. To achieve such a smooth loss function, we take the quadratic loss, as follows:

$$\left(y - y^{predicted}\right)^2$$

Again, readers should note that the quadratic cost function is only one method, and there are many other ways to define loss. Eventually, the purpose of choosing different loss functions is to get

1. A smoothed partial derivative with respect to weight

2. A good convex curve, to achieve global minimum. However, a lot of other factors come into play while finding a global minimum (learning rate, shape of function, etc.).

We'd randomly choose a starting point for an (imaginary) ball and then simulate the motion of the ball as it rolls down to the bottom of the valley. In a similar analogy, imagine that we initialize the weights of the network or, in general, the parameters of a function, at some arbitrary point on a curve (just like dropping a ball on any point of the slope), and then we check the slope (derivative) nearby.

We know that the ball will go down in the direction of maximum slope, owing to gravity. Similarly, we move the weights in the direction of derivative at that point and update the weights according to following rule:

Let $J(w)$ = Cost as a function of weights

w = Parameters of the network ($v1$ and $v2$)

w_i= Initial set of weights (random initialization)

$$ w_{updated} = w_i - \eta \, dJ(w) / dw $$

Here, $dJ(w)/dw$ = partial derivative of weight, w, with respect to $J(w)$

η = learning rate.

The *learning rate* is more of a hyper parameter, and there is no fixed way to find the most appropriate learning rate. However, one can always look into the batch-loss to find it.

One way is to see the loss and analyze the pattern of loss. In general, a bad learning rate leads to erratic loss on mini-batches. It (loss) can go up and down recursively, without stabilizing.

Figure 1-18 illustrates a better intuitive explanation, supported by a graph.

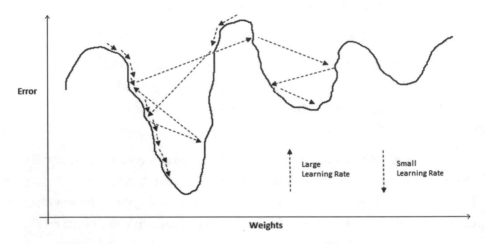

Figure 1-18. *Impact of small and large learning rates*

In the preceding diagram, there are two cases present:

1. Small learning rate

2. Large learning rate

The purpose is to reach the minimum of the preceding graph, and we must reach the bottom of the valley (as in the ball analogy). Now the learning rate is related to the jump the ball makes while rolling down the hill.

Considering case 1 first (the left part of the diagram), in which we make small jumps, gradually keep rolling down, slowly, and eventually reaching the minimum, there is a chance that the ball may get stuck in some small crevice along the way and isn't able to get escape it, because of its inability to make large jumps.

In case 2 (the right part of the diagram), there is a larger learning rate, as compared to the slope of the curvature. This is a suboptimal strategy that might actually eject us from the valley, in some cases, which could be a good start to coming out of the reach of local minima but not at all satisfactory in the event that we skip the global minima.

In the diagram, we are achieving a local minima, but this is just one case. What this means is that the weights get stuck at local minima, and we miss out on global minima. Gradient descent, or stochastic gradient descent, doesn't guarantee convergence to the global minima for neural networks (assuming hidden units are not linear), because the cost functions are non-convex.

An ideal situation is one in which step size keeps on changing and is more adaptive in nature, with a little higher at the start, then gradually decreasing over a period of time, until convergence.

Backpropagation

Understanding the backpropagation algorithm can take some time, and if you are looking for a fast implementation of a neural network, then you can skip this section, as modern libraries have the capability to auto-differentiate and perform the entire training procedure. However, understanding this algorithm would definitely give you insights into problems related to deep learning (learning problems, slow learning, exploding gradients, diminishing gradients).

Gradient descent is a powerful algorithm, yet it is a slow method when the number of weights increases. In the case of neural networks having parameters in the range of thousands, training each weight with respect to the loss function or, rather, formulating the loss as a function of all the weights becomes painstakingly slow and extremely complex to use for practical purposes.

Thanks to the path-breaking paper by Geoffrey Hinton and his colleagues in 1986, we have an extremely fast and beautiful algorithm that helps us to find the partial derivative of the loss with respect to each weight. This algorithm is the workhorse of the training procedure for every

deep learning algorithm. More detailed information can be found here:
`www.cs.toronto.edu/~hinton/backprop.html`.

It is the most efficient possible procedure to compute the exact
gradient, and its computational cost is always of the same $O(\ )$ complexity
as computing the loss itself. The proof of backpropagation is beyond the
scope of this book; however, the intuitive explanation of the algorithm can
give you an excellent insight into its complex working.

For backpropagation to work, two basic assumptions are taken
regarding the `Error` function.

1. Total error can be written as a summation of
    individual error of training samples/minibatch,
    $E = \Sigma E_x$

2. Error can be written as a function of outputs of the
    network

Backpropagation consists of two parts:

1. **Forward pass**, wherein we initialize the weights and
    make a feedforward network to store all the values

2. **Backward pass**, which is performed to have the
    stored values update the weights

Partial derivatives, chain rules, and linear algebra are the main tools
required to deal with backpropagation (Figure 1-19).

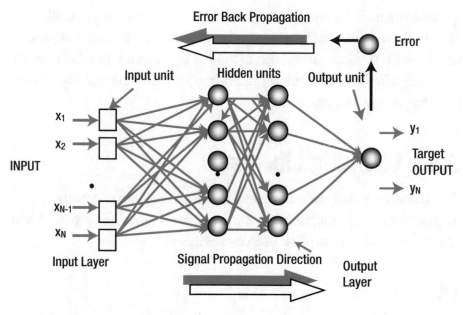

Figure 1-19. *Backpropagation mechanism in an ANN*

Initially, all the edge weights are randomly assigned. For every input in the training dataset, the ANN is activated, and its output is observed. This output is compared with the desired output that we already know, and the error is "propagated" back to the previous layer. This error is noted, and the weights are "adjusted" accordingly. This process is repeated until the output error is below a predetermined threshold.

Once the preceding algorithm terminates, we have a "learned" ANN, which we consider to be ready to work with "new" inputs. This ANN is said to have learned from several examples (labeled data) and from its mistakes (error propagation).

Curious readers should investigate the original paper on backpropagation. We have provided a list of resources and blogs to understand the algorithm in greater depth. However, when it comes to implementation, you will hardly write your own code on backpropagation, as most of the libraries support automatic differentiation, and you won't really want to tweak the backpropagation algorithm.

In layman's language, in backpropagation, we try to sequentially update the weights, first by making a forward pass on the network, after which we first update the weights of the last layer, using the label and last layer outputs, then subsequently use this information recursively on the layer just before and proceed.

Deep Learning Libraries

This section involves an introduction to the some of the widely used deep learning libraries, including Theano, TensorFlow, and Keras, also in addition to a basic tutorial on each one of these.

Theano

Theano was an open source project primarily developed at the Université de Montréal under the supervision of Yoshua Bengio. It is a numerical computation library for Python with syntaxes similar to NumPy. It is efficient at performing complex mathematical expressions with multidimensional arrays. This makes it is a perfect choice for neural networks.

The link `http://deeplearning.net/software/theano` will give the user a better idea of the various operations involved. We will be illustrating the installation steps for Theano on different platforms, followed by the basic tutorials involved.

Theano is a mathematical library that provides ways to create the machine learning models that could be used later for multiple datasets. Many tools have been implemented on top of Theano. Principally, it includes

- Blocks `http://blocks.readthedocs.org/en/latest/`

- Keras `http://keras.io/`

- Lasagne http://lasagne.readthedocs.org/en/latest/

- PyLearn2 http://deeplearning.net/software/pylearn2/

Note   It should be noted that at the time of writing this book, contributions to the Theano package have been stopped by the community members, owing to a substantial increase in the usage of other deep learning packages.

Theano Installation

The following command will work like a charm for Theano installation on Ubuntu:

```
> sudo apt-get install python-numpy python-scipy python-dev
python-pip python-nose g++ libopenblas-dev git

> sudo pip install Theano
```

For detailed instructions on installing Theano on different platforms, please refer to the following link: http://deeplearning.net/software/theano/install.html. Even docker images with CPU and GPU compatibility are available.

Note   It is always advisable to proceed with installation in a separate virtual environment.

The latest version of Theano can be installed from the development version available at

```
> git clone git://github.com/Theano/Theano.git
> cd Theano
> python setup.py install
```

For the installation on Windows, take the following steps (sourced from an answer on Stack Overflow):

1. Install TDM GCC x64 (http://tdm-gcc.tdragon.net/).

2. Install Anaconda x64 (www.continuum.io/ downloads, say in C:/Anaconda).

3. After Anaconda installation, run the following commands:

   a. `conda update conda`

   b. `conda update -all`

   c. `conda install mingw libpython`

4. Include the destination `'C:\Anaconda\Scripts'` in the environment variable PATH.

5. Install Theano, either the older version or the latest version available.

   a. Older version:

      ```
      > pip install Theano
      ```

   b. Latest version:

      ```
      > pip install --upgrade --no-deps git+git://
      github.com/Theano/Theano.git
      ```

Theano Examples

The following section introduces the basic codes in the Theano library. The Tensor subpackage of the Theano library contains most of the required symbols.

The following example makes use of the Tensor subpackage and performs operations on the two numbers (outputs have been included for reference):

```
> import theano
> import theano.tensor as T
> import numpy
> from theano import function
# Variables 'x' and 'y' are defined
> x = T.dscalar('x')                  # dscalar : Theano datatype
> y = T.dscalar('y')

# 'x' and 'y' are instances of TensorVariable, and are of
dscalar theano type
> type(x)
<class 'theano.tensor.var.TensorVariable'>
> x.type
TensorType(float64, scalar)
> T.dscalar
TensorType(float64, scalar)

# 'z' represents the sum of 'x' and 'y' variables. Theano's pp
function, pretty-print out, is used to display the computation
of the variable 'z'
> z = x + y
> from theano import pp
> print(pp(z))
(x+y)
```

```
# 'f' is a numpy.ndarray of zero dimensions, which takes input
as the first argument, and output as the second argument
# 'f' is being compiled in C code
> f = function([x, y], z)
```

The preceding function could be used in the following manner to perform the addition operation:

```
> f(6, 10)
array(16.0)
> numpy.allclose(f(10.3, 5.4), 15.7)
True
```

TensorFlow

TensorFlow is an open sourced library by Google for large-scale machine learning implementations. TensorFlow, in a true sense, is the successor of DistBelief, which was an earlier software framework released by Google capable of utilizing computing clusters with thousands of machines to train large models.

TensorFlow is the brainchild of the software engineers and researchers from the Google Brain Team, which is part of the Google group (now Alphabet) and is primarily focused on deep learning and its applications. It makes use of the data flow graphs for the numerical computation, mentioned in detail following. It has been designed in such a way that computations on CPUs or GPU systems across a single desktop or servers or mobile devices are catered to by a single API.

TensorFlow offers the movement of highly intensive computational tasks from CPUs to heterogeneous GPU-oriented platforms, with very minute changes in the codes. Also, a model trained on one machine could be used on another light device, such as an Android-enabled mobile device, for final implementation purposes.

TensorFlow is the foundation for the implementation of such applications as DeepDream, which is an automated image-captioning software, and RankBrain, which helps Google to process search results and provide more relevant search results to users.

To get a better sense of the working and implementation of TensorFlow, one can read the relevant white paper at `http://download.tensorflow.org/paper/whitepaper2015.pdf`.

Data Flow Graphs

Data flow graphs are used by TensorFlow to represent the mathematical computations performed in the form of graphs. It makes use of the directed graphs, with nodes and edges. The nodes represent mathematical operations and act as a terminal for data input, output of results, or read/write of persistent variables. The edges handle the input and output relationships between nodes. The data edges carry tensors, or dynamically sized multidimensional data arrays, between the nodes. The movement of these tensor units through the whole graph has itself lead to the name *TensorFlow*. The nodes in a graph, upon receiving all their respective tensors from the incoming edges, execute asynchronously and in parallel.

The overall design and flow of computations covered within a data flow graph occur in a session and are then executed on the desired machines. TensorFlow, with the Python, C, and C+ APIs offered, relies on C++ for optimized computations.

With the following features of TensorFlow, it is the best choice for the massive parallelism and high scalability required in the field of machine learning

- *Deep flexibility*: Users get the full privilege to write their own libraries on top of the TensorFlow. One need only create the whole computation in the form of a graph, and the rest is taken care of by TensorFlow.

- *True portability*: Extensibility offered by TensorFlow enables a machine learning code written on a laptop to be trained on GPUs for faster model training, with no code changes, and to be deployed on mobile, in the final product, or on docker, as a cloud service.

- *Automatic differentiation*: TensorFlow handles the derivatives computation for the gradient-based machine learning algorithms by the automatic differentiation functionality of it. The computation of derivatives of values helps in understanding the extended graph of values with respect to each other.

- *Language options*: TensorFlow offers Python and C++ interfaces to build and execute the computational graphs.

- *Performance maximization*: The compute elements from the TensorFlow graph can be assigned to multiple devices, and TensorFlow takes care of the maximum performance by its wide support of threads, queues, and asynchronous computation.

TensorFlow Installation

TensorFlow installation is very easy, like any other Python package, and can be achieved by using a single pip install command. Also, if required, users can follow the detailed explanation for the installation on the main site of TensorFlow (`www.tensorflow.org/versions/r0.10/get_started/os_setup.html`, for the r0.10 version).

Installation via pip must be preceded by the binary package installation relevant to the platform. Please refer to the following link for more details on the TensorFlow package and its repository `https://github.com/tensorflow/tensorflow`.

To check the installation of TensorFlow on Windows, check out the following blog link: `www.hanselman.com/blog/ PlayingWithTensorFlowOnWindows.aspx`.

TensorFlow Examples

Running and experimenting with TensorFlow is as easy as the installation. The tutorial on the official web site, `www.tensorflow.org/`, is pretty clear and covers basic to expert-level examples.

Following is one such example, with the basics of TensorFlow (outputs have been included for reference):

```
> import tensorflow as tf
> hello = tf.constant('Hello, Tensors!')
> sess = tf.Session()
> sess.run(hello)
Hello, Tensors!

# Mathematical computation
> a = tf.constant(10)
> b = tf.constant(32)
> sess.run(a+b)
42
```

The `run()` method takes the resulting variables for computations as arguments, and a backward chain of required calls are made for this.

TensorFlow graphs get formed from nodes not requiring any kind of input, i.e., the source. These nodes then pass their output to further nodes, which perform computations on the resulting tensors, and the whole process moves in this pattern.

The following examples show the creation of two matrices using Numpy, then using TensorFlow to assign these matrices as objects in TensorFlow, and then multiplying both the matrices. The second example includes the addition and subtraction of two constants. A TensorFlow session has also been activated to perform the operation and deactivated once the operation is complete.

```
> import tensorflow as tf
> import numpy as np

> mat_1 = 10*np.random.random_sample((3, 4))    # Creating NumPy
                                                   arrays
> mat_2 = 10*np.random.random_sample((4, 6))

# Creating a pair of constant ops, and including the above made
matrices
> tf_mat_1 = tf.constant(mat_1)
> tf_mat_2 = tf.constant(mat_2)

# Multiplying TensorFlow matrices with matrix multiplication
operation
> tf_mat_prod = tf.matmul(tf_mat_1 , tf_mat_2)

> sess = tf.Session()              # Launching a session

# run() executes required ops and performs the request to store
output in 'mult_matrix' variable
> mult_matrix = sess.run(tf_mat_prod)
> print(mult_matrix)

# Performing constant operations with the addition and
subtraction of two constants
> a = tf.constant(10)
> a = tf.constant(20)

> print("Addition of constants 10 and 20 is %i " % sess.
run(a+b))
```

```
Addition of constants 10 and 20 is 30
> print("Subtraction of constants 10 and 20 is %i " % sess.
run(a-b))
Subtraction of constants 10 and 20 is -10

> sess.close()                          # Closing the session
```

Note   As no graph was specified in the preceding example with the
TensorFlow, the session makes use of the default instance only.

Keras

Keras is a highly modular neural networks library, which runs on top of
Theano or TensorFlow. Keras is one of the libraries which supports both
CNNs and RNNs (we will be discussing these two neural networks in detail
in later chapters), and runs effortlessly on GPU and CPU.

A model is understood as a sequence or a graph of standalone,
fully configurable modules that can be plugged together with as little
restrictions as possible. In particular, neural layers, cost functions,
optimizers, initialization schemes, activation functions, regularization
schemes are all standalone modules that could be combined to create new
models.

Keras Installation

In addition to the Theano or TensorFlow as back end, Keras makes use
of the few libraries as dependencies. Installing these before Theano or
TensorFlow installation eases the process.

```
> pip install numpy scipy
> pip install scikit-learn
> pip install pillow
> pip install h5py
```

> **Note**   Keras always require the latest version of Theano to be installed (as mentioned in the previous section). We have made use of TensorFlow as back end for Keras throughout the book.

```
> pip install keras
```

Keras Principles

Keras offers a model as one of its main data structures. Each model is a customizable entity that can be made up of different layers, cost functions, activation functions, and regularization schemes. Keras offers a wide range of pre-built layers to plug in a neural network, a few of which include convolutional, dropout, pooling, locally connected, recurrent, noise, and normalization layers. An individual layer of the network is considered to be an input object for the next layer.

Built primarily for the implementation of neural networks and deep learning, code snippets in Keras will be included in later chapters as well, in addition to their relevant neural networks.

Keras Examples

The base data structure of Keras is a model type, made up of the different layers of the network. The sequential model is the major type of model in Keras, in which layers are added one by one until the final output layer.

The following example of Keras uses the blood transfusion dataset from the UCI ML Repository. One can find the details regarding the data

here: https://archive.ics.uci.edu/ml/datasets/Blood+Transfusion+
Service+Center). The data is taken from a blood transfusion service
center located in Taiwan and has four attributes, in addition to the target
variable. The problem is one of binary classification, with '1' standing for
the person who has donated the blood and '0' for the person who refused
a blood donation. More details regarding the attributes can be gleaned
from the link mentioned.

Save the dataset shared at the web site in the current working directory
(if possible, with the headers removed). We start by loading the dataset,
building a basic MLP model in Keras, followed by fitting the model on the
dataset.

The basic type of model in Keras is sequential, which offers layer-
by-layer addition of complexity to the model. The multiple layers can be
fabricated with their respective configurations and stacked onto the initial
base model.

```
# Importing the required libraries and layers and model from
Keras
> import keras
> from keras.layers import Dense
> from keras.models import Sequential
> import numpy as np

# Dataset Link : # https://archive.ics.uci.edu/ml/datasets/Blood
+Transfusion+Service+Center
# Save the dataset as a .csv file :

tran_ = np.genfromtxt('transfusion.csv', delimiter=',')
X=tran_[:,0:4]            # The dataset offers 4 input variables
Y=tran_[:,4]             # Target variable with '1' and '0'
print(x)
```

As the input data has four corresponding variables, the input_dim, which refers to the number of different input variables, has been set to four. We have made use of the fully connected layers defined by dense layers in Keras to build the additional layers. The selection of the network structure is done on the basis of the complexity of the problem. Here, the first hidden layer is made up of eight neurons, which are responsible for further capturing the nonlinearity. The layer has been initialized with the uniformly distributed random numbers and with the activation function as ReLU, as described previously in this chapter. The second layer has six neurons and configurations similar to its previous layer.

```
# Creating our first MLP model with Keras
> mlp_keras = Sequential()
> mlp_keras.add(Dense(8, input_dim=4, init='uniform',
activation='relu'))
> mlp_keras.add(Dense(6, init='uniform', activation='relu'))
```

In the last layer of output, we have set the activation as sigmoid, mentioned previously, which is responsible for generating a value between 0 and 1 and helps in the binary classification.

```
> mlp_keras.add(Dense(1, init='uniform', activation='sigmoid'))
```

To compile the network, we have made use of the binary classification with logarithmic loss and selected Adam as the default choice of optimizer, and accuracy as the desired metric to be tracked. The network is trained using the backpropagation algorithm, along with the given optimization algorithm and loss function.

```
> mlp_keras.compile(loss = 'binary_crossentropy',
optimizer='adam',metrics=['accuracy'])
```

The model has been trained on the given dataset with a small number of iterations (nb_epoch) and started with a feasible batch size of instances (batch_size). The parameters could be chosen either on the basis of prior experience of working with such kinds of datasets, or one can even make use of Grid Search to optimize the choice of such parameters. We will be covering the same concept in later chapters, where necessary.

```
> mlp_keras.fit(X,Y, nb_epoch=200, batch_size=8, verbose=0)
```

The next step is to finally evaluate the model that has been built and to check out the performance metrics, loss, and accuracy on the initial training dataset. The same operation could be performed on a new test dataset with which the model is not acquainted and could be a better measure of the model performance.

```
> accuracy = mlp_keras.evaluate(X,Y)
> print("Accuracy : %.2f%% " % (accuracy[1]*100 ))
```

If one wants to further optimize the model by using different combinations of parameters and other tweaks, it could be done by using different parameters and steps while undertaking model creation and validation, though it need not result in better performance in all cases.

```
# Using a different set of optimizer
> from keras.optimizers import SGD
> opt = SGD(lr=0.01)
```

The following creates a model with configurations similar to those in the earlier model but with a different optimizer and including a validation dataset from the initial training data:

```
> mlp_optim = Sequential()
> mlp_optim.add(Dense(8, input_dim=4, init='uniform',
activation='relu'))
> mlp_optim.add(Dense(6, init='uniform', activation='relu'))
```

```
> mlp_optim.add(Dense(1, init='uniform', activation='sigmoid'))

# Compiling the model with SGD
> mlp_optim.compile(loss = 'binary_crossentropy',
optimizer=opt, metrics=['accuracy'])

# Fitting the model and checking accuracy
> mlp_optim.fit(X,Y, validation_split=0.3, nb_epoch=150,
batch_size=10, verbose=0)
> results_optim = mlp_optim.evaluate(X,Y)
> print("Accuracy : %.2f%%" % (results_optim[1]*100 ) )
```

Make sure that all the packages mentioned for natural language processing and deep learning in the preceding sections are installed before moving forward. Once you have set up the system, you will be good to go with the examples offered throughout this book.

Next Steps

This first chapter presented an introduction to the fields of natural language processing and deep learning and related introductory examples from the publicly available Python libraries. We will be delving deeper into this in the next chapters, introducing current industry-wide problems in natural language processing and how the presence of deep learning has impacted the paradigm of solving these in an efficient manner.

CHAPTER 2

Word Vector Representations

When dealing with languages and words, we might end up classifying texts across thousands of classes, for use in multiple natural language processing (NLP) tasks. Much research has been undertaken in this field in recent years, and this has resulted in the transformation of words in languages to the format of vectors that can be used in multiple sets of algorithms and processes. This chapter offers an in-depth explanation of word embeddings and their effectiveness. We introduce their origin and compare the different models used to accomplish various NLP tasks.

Introduction to Word Embedding

The categorization and quantifying of semantic similarities among linguistic items comes under the rubric of distributional semantics and is based on their distribution in the usage of a language. Vector space models, signifying text documents and queries in the form of vectors, have long been used for distributional semantics purposes. The representation of words in an N-dimensional vector space by vector space models is useful for different NLP algorithms to achieve better results, as it leads to groupings of similar text in the new vector space.

© Palash Goyal, Sumit Pandey, Karan Jain 2018
P. Goyal, et al., *Deep Learning for Natural Language Processing*,
https://doi.org/10.1007/978-1-4842-3685-7_2

The term *word embedding* was coined by Yoshua Bengio in his paper "A Neural Probabilistic Language Model" (`www.jmlr.org/papers/volume3/bengio03a/bengio03a.pdf`). This was followed by Ronan Collobert and Jason Weston in their paper "A Unified Architecture for Natural Language Processing" (`https://ronan.collobert.com/pub/matos/2008_nlp_icml.pdf`), in which the authors demonstrated how the use of multitask learning and semi-supervised learning improve the generalization of shared tasks. Finally, Tomas Mikolov et al., who created word2vec and put word embeddings under the lens, elucidated the training for word embeddings and also the use of pretrained word embeddings. Later, Jeffrey Pennington introduced GloVe, another set of pretrained word embeddings.

Word embeddings models have proven to be more efficient than the bag-of-word models or one-hot-encoding schemes, made up of sparse vectors with a size equivalent to that of the vocabulary, used initially. The sparsity present in vectoral representation was an outcome of the vastness of the vocabulary and labeling of the word or document in it at the index position. Word embedding has replaced this concept by making use of the surrounding words of all the individual words, using the information present from the given text and passing it to the model. This has allowed embedding to take the form of a dense vector, which, in a continuous vector space, represents the projection of the individual words. Embedding thus refers to the coordinates of the word in the newly learned vector space.

The following example presents the creation of a word vector, using the one-hot encoding for the words present in the sample vocabulary, followed by the reformation of the word vectors. It uses a distributed representation approach and shows how the final vector composition can be used to infer the relation between the words.

Let's assume that our vocabulary contains the words, *Rome, Italy, Paris, France,* and *country.* We can make use of each of these words to create a representation, using a one-hot scheme for all the words, as shown for *Rome* in Figure 2-1.

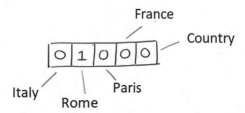

Figure 2-1. *A representation of Rome*

Using the preceding approach of presenting the words in vector form, we can more or less make use only of testing the equality between the words, by comparing their vectors. This approach will not serve other, higher purposes. In a better form of representation, we can create multiple hierarchies or segments, in which the information shown by each of the words can be assigned various weightages. The selection of these segments or dimensions could be of our choice, and each of the words will be represented by a distribution of weights across these segments. So, now we have a new format of word representation, using different scales for each of the words (Figure 2-2).

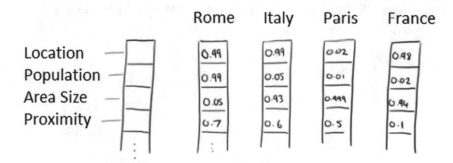

Figure 2-2. *Our representation*

The preceding vectors used for each word does signify the actual meaning of the word and provides a better scale with which to make a comparison across the words. The newly formed vectors are sufficiently capable of answering the kind of relationships being held among words. Figure 2-3 represents the vectors being formed using this new approach.

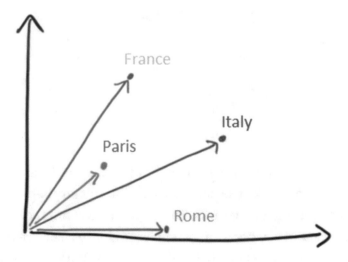

Figure 2-3. *Our vectors*

The output vectors for different words does retain the linguistic regularities and patterns, and this is proven by the linear translations of these patterns. For example, the result of the difference between the vectors and the words following, vector(*France*) - vector(*Paris*) + vector(*Italy*), will be close to vector(*Rome*), as shown in Figure 2-4.

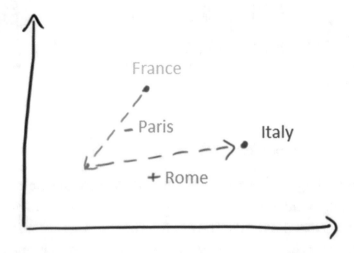

Figure 2-4. *Comparing vectors*

Over time, word embeddings have emerged to become one of the most important applications of the unsupervised learning domain. The semantic relationships offered by word vectors have helped in the NLP approaches of neural machine translation, information retrieval, and question-and-answer applications.

Neural Language Model

The feedforward neural net language model (FNNLM) proposed by Bengio introduces a feedforward neural network consisting of a single hidden layer that predicts the future words, in our example, only a single word, of the sequence.

The neural net language model is trained to find θ, which maximizes the training corpus penalized log-likelihood:

$$L = \frac{1}{T}\sum_t \log f\left(w_t, w_{t-1}, \ldots, w_{t-n+1} ; \theta\right) + R(\theta)$$

Here, f is the composite function made up of the parameters related to distributed feature vectors of each of the words present in the vocabulary and parameters of the feedforward or recurrent neural network. $R(\theta)$ refers to the regularization term, which applies a weight decay penalty to the weights of the neural network and the feature vectors matrix. The function f returns the probability score computed by the softmax function for the word at the t-th position, using the previous n words.

The models introduced by Bengio were among the first of their kind and laid the foundation of future word embedding models. The components of these original models are still used across current word embedding models. Some of these components include the following:

1. **Embedding layer**: This keeps a record of the representation of all the words in the training dataset. It is initialized with a set of random weights. The embedding layer is made up of three parts,

which include the size of the vocabulary, the output size of the vector in which all the words will be embedded, and the length of the input sequences to the model. The resulting output of an embedding layer is a two-dimensional vector, which has the final embedding for all the words present in the given sequence of words.

2. **Intermediate layer(s)**: The hidden layers, ranging from initial to final layers and with a count of one or more, that produce the representation of the input text data by applying the nonlinear functions in the neural network on the word embeddings of the previous n-words.

3. **Softmax layer**: This is the final layer of the neural network architecture and returns a probability distribution over all the words present in the input vocabulary.

Bengio's paper mentions the computation cost involved in the softmax normalization and that it is proportional to the vocabulary size. This has created challenges in trials of new algorithms for neural language models and word embedding models on the full vocabulary size.

The neural net language models have helped to attain generalization for words that are not present in the current vocabulary, as a sequence of words that has never been seen before is given higher probability if the combination of words is similar to the words that have already been included in a sentence.

Word2vec

Word2vec, or word-to-vector, models were introduced by Tomas Mikolov et al. (https://arxiv.org/pdf/1301.3781.pdf) and are one of the most adopted models. It is used to learn the word embeddings, or vector representation of words. The paper compares the performance of the proposed models with previous models, by checking the similarity between groups of words. The techniques proposed in the paper resulted in the vector representation of words with similarity across multiple degrees for similar words. The similarity of the word representation goes beyond the simple syntactic regularities, with simple algebraic operations also being performed on the word vectors.

Word2vec models make use internally of a simple neural network of a single layer and capture the weights of the hidden layer. The aim of training the model is to learn the weights of the hidden layer, which represents the "word embeddings." Although word2vec uses neural network architecture, the architecture itself is not complex enough and doesn't make use of any kind of nonlinearities. It can be discharged of the label of deep learning for now.

Word2vec offers a range of models that are used to represent words in an n-dimensional space in such a way that similar words and words representing closer meanings are placed close to one another. This justifies the whole exercise of placing words in a new vector space. We will go through the two most frequently used models, skip-gram and continuous bag-of-words (CBOW), followed by their implementation in TensorFlow. Both models are similar algorithmically, with the difference being only in the way they perform the prediction. The CBOW model predicts the center words by making use of the context or surrounding words, and the skip-gram model predicts the context words using the center words.

In comparison with the one-hot encoding, word2vec helps in reducing the size of the encoding space and compresses the representation of words to the desired length for the vector (Figure 2-5). Word2vec approaches word representation on the basis of the context in which words are presented. For example, synonyms, opposites, semantically similar concepts, and similar words are present in similar contexts across a text and, thus, are embedded in similar fashion, and their final embeddings lie closer to one another.

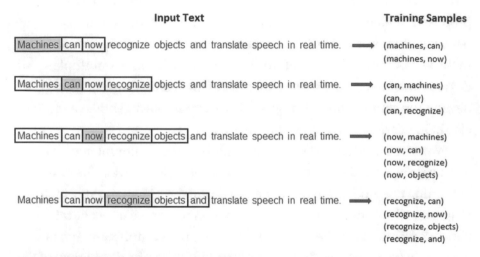

Figure 2-5. *Using the window size of 2 to pick the words from the sentence "Machines can now recognize objects and translate speech in real time" and training the model*

Skip-Gram Model

A skip-gram model predicts the surrounding words by using the current word in the sequence. The classification score of the surrounding words is based on the syntactic relation and occurrences with the center word. Any word present in the sequence is taken as input to the log-linear classifier, which in turn makes a prediction of the words falling under a certain pre-specified range of words occurring before and after the center word. There is a trade-off between the selection of the range of words and the computation complexity and quality of the resulting word vectors. As the distance to the concerned word increases, the distant words are related on lower level with the current word, as compared to the closer words. This is tackled by assigning the weights as a function of the distance from the center words and giving lesser weights, or sampling fewer words, from the words at higher ranges (see Figure 2-6).

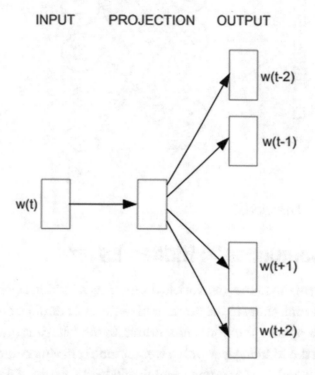

Figure 2-6. *Skip-gram model architecture*

The training of the skip-gram model doesn't involve dense matrix multiplications. Coupled with a bit of optimization, it could result in a highly efficient training process for the model.

Model Components: Architecture

In this example, the network is used to train the model, with the input word fed as a one-hot-encoded vector and the output as a one-hot-encoded vector representing the output word (Figure 2-7).

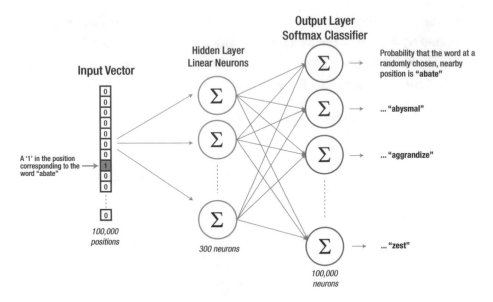

Figure 2-7. *The model*

Model Components: Hidden Layer

The training of the neural network is done using a hidden layer, with the count of neurons equal to the number of features or dimensions by which we want to represent the word embedding. In the following graph, we have represented the hidden layer with a weight matrix having columns of 300, equal to the number of neurons—which will be the count of the features in the final output vector of word embedding—and rows as 100,000, which is equal to the size of the vocabulary used to train the model.

The number of neurons is considered as a hyper-parameter of the model and could be changed as required. The model trained by Google makes use of 300 dimensional feature vectors, and it has been made public. It could be a good start for those who don't want to train their set of models for word embeddings. You may use the following link to download the trained set of vectors: `https://code.google.com/archive/p/word2vec/`.

As the input vectors given as input for each of the words in the vocabulary are one-hot encoded, the computations happening in the hidden layer stage will make sure that only the vector corresponding to the respective words is selected from the weight matrix and passed on to the output layer. As shown in Figure 2-8, in the case of vocabulary of size v, for any word, there will be "1" present at the desired index in the input vector, and after multiplying it with the weight matrix, for each of the words, we will get the corresponding row of the word as the output vector. Thus, what really matters is not the output but the weight matrix. Figure 2-8 represents clearly how the weight matrix of the hidden layer is used to calculate the word vector lookup table.

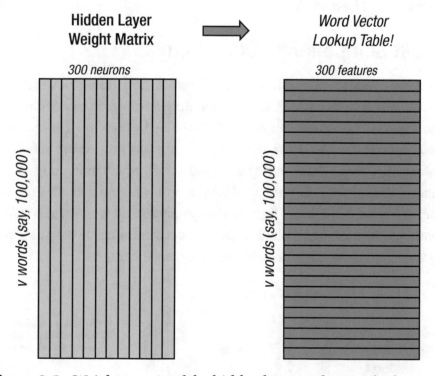

Figure 2-8. *Weight matrix of the hidden layer and vector lookup table*

Even though the one-hot-encoded vector is made up entirely of zeros, multiplying a 1 × 100,000 dimension vector with a 100,000 × 300 weight matrix will still result in the selection of the corresponding row where "1" is present. Figure 2-9 gives the pictorial representation of this calculation, and the output of the hidden layer is the vector representation of the concerned word.

$$
[0\ 0\ 0\ ...\ 0\ 1\ 0\ 0] \times
\begin{bmatrix}
14 & 22 & 3 & ... & 13 & 22 & 27 & 22 \\
14 & 11 & 6 & ... & 28 & 12 & 25 & 25 \\
4 & 8 & 22 & ... & 11 & 24 & 24 & 12 \\
... & ... & ... & ... & ... & ... & ... & ... \\
18 & 26 & 1 & ... & 11 & 8 & 25 & 19 \\
25 & 24 & 17 & ... & 9 & 8 & 14 & 3 \\
26 & 0 & 18 & ... & 17 & 12 & 16 & 18 \\
16 & 22 & 3 & ... & 4 & 18 & 17 & 8
\end{bmatrix}
= [25\ \ 24\ \ 17\ \ ...\ \ 9\ \ 8\ \ 14\ \ 3]
$$

Figure 2-9. *The calculation*

Model Components: Output Layer

Our main intention behind calculating the word embedding for words is to make sure that words with similar meanings lie closer in our defined vector space. This issue is automatically handled by the model, because words with similar meanings, in most cases, are surrounded by similar contexts (i.e., words surrounding the input word), which inherently makes the weight adjustment in a similar manner during the training process (Figure 2-10). In addition to the synonyms and words with similar meanings, the model also handles the cases of stemming, as the plural or singular words (say, *car* and *cars*) will have similar contexts.

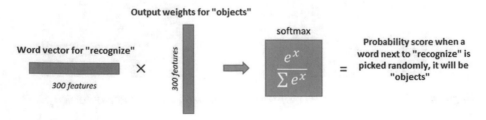

Figure 2-10. *The training process*

CBOW Model

The continuous bag-of-words model shares an architectural similarity to the FNNLM, as shown in Figure 2-11. The order of words doesn't impact the projection layer, and what's important is which words are currently falling in the *bag* to make the output word prediction.

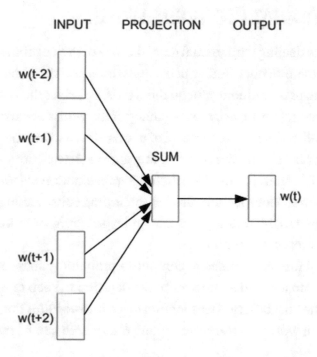

Figure 2-11. *Continuous bag-of-words model architecture*

The input and the projection layers share the weight matrix for all word positions in a way similar to that shared in the FNNLM. The CBOW model makes use of the continuous distribution representation of the context, thus a *continuous* bag of words.

Note   Using CBOW over smaller datasets results in smoothening of the distributional information, as the model treats the entire context as a single observation.

Subsampling Frequent Words

In most cases dealing with textual data, the size of the vocabulary can increase to a significant number of unique words and could be composed of different sizes of frequency for all the words. To select the words to be kept for modeling purposes, the frequency of the words occurring in the corpus is used to decide the removal of words, by checking the count of overall words as well. The subsampling approach was introduced by Mikolov et al. in their paper "Distributed Representations of Words and Phrases and their Compositionality." By including subsampling, significant speed is gained in the training process, and word representations are learned in a more regular manner.

A survival function is used to compute a probability score at the word level, which can be used later to make the decision to keep or remove the word from the vocabulary. The function takes into account the frequency of the relevant word and the subsampling rate, which can be tweaked:

$$P(w_i) = \left(\sqrt{\frac{z(w_i)}{s}} + 1 \right) \frac{s}{z(w_i)}$$

where, w_i is the work concerned, $z(w_i)$ is the frequency of the word in the training dataset or corpus, and s is the subsampling rate.

Note   The original function mentioned by Mikolov et al. in their paper is different from the one used in the actual implementation of the word2vec code and has been mentioned in the preceding text. The formula chosen in the paper for subsampling was chosen heuristically, and it includes a threshold, *t*, which is rendered typically as 10^{-5}, as the minimum frequency of the words in the corpus. The formula mentioned in the paper for subsampling is

$$P(w_i) = 1 - \left(\sqrt{\frac{t}{f(w_i)}} \right)$$

where, w_i is the word concerned, $f(w_i)$ is the frequency of the word in the training dataset or corpus, and *s* is the threshold used.

The subsampling rate makes the key decision on whether to keep the frequent words. A smaller value means the words are less likely to be kept in the corpus for model training. In most cases, a preferred threshold is put over the output of the survival function to remove the words occurring less frequently. The preferred value is 0.001 for the parameter *s*. The subsampling approach mentioned helps in countering the imbalance between the rare and frequent words across the corpus.

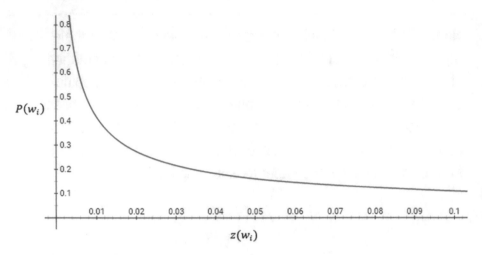

Figure 2-12. *Distribution of the Survival function,*
P(x) = {(sqrt(x/0.001) + 1) * (0.001/x)} for a constant value of 0.001
for sampling rate (Credits : http://www.mccormickml.com)

The figure displays the graph between the frequency of the word
with the final probability score generated by the sub-sampling approach.
As none of the word present in corpus can occupy a higher percentage,
so we will consider the part of the graph with the lower ranges of the
percentage of word, i.e., along x-axis. There are few observations which
we can derive from the above chart regarding the percentage of the words
and their relation with the scores being generated, thereby the impact of
subsampling on words:

- $P(w_i) = 1$ occurs for the cases when $z(w_i) < = 0.0026$. It
  means that the words with their frequency percentage
  lesser than 0.26% will not be considered for the
  subsampling.

- $P(w_i) = 0.5$ occurs for the cases when $z(w_i) = 0.00746$.
  Thus the percentage required for a word to have 50%
  chance of being kept or removed is when it has 0.746%
  frequency.

- $P(w_i) = 0.033$ occurs for the cases when $z(w_i) = 1$, i.e., even when the whole corpus is comprised of a single word only, there is 96.7% probability of it getting removed from the corpus, which doesn't make any sense practically.

Negative Sampling

Negative sampling is a simplified form of the noise contrastive estimation (NCE) approach, as it makes certain assumptions while selecting the count of the *noise*, or *negative*, samples, and their distribution. It is used as an alternative to the hierarchical softmax function. Although negative sampling is used at the time of training the model, at the time of inference, the full softmax value is to be calculated, to obtain a normalized probability score.

The size of the weight matrix in the hidden layer of the neural network model is dependent on the overall size of the vocabulary, which is of higher orders. This results in a huge number of weight parameters. All the weight parameters are updated in multiple iterations of millions and billions of training samples. Negative sampling causes the model to update weights by only a small percentage, for each of the training samples.

The input representation of words given to model is by a one-hot-encoded vector. Negative sampling randomly selects a given number of "negative" words (say, 10) for which the weights are updated with the weights of the "positive" word (or center word). In total, for 11 words (10 + 1), the weights will be updated. With reference to the figure given previously, any iteration will result in updating $11 \times 300 = 3,300$ values in the weight matrix. However, irrespective of the usage of the negative sampling, weights of only "positive" words are updated in the hidden layer.

The probability for the selection of the "negative" samples depends on the frequency of the word in the corpus. The higher the frequency, the higher will be the probability of the "negative" word being selected.

As mentioned in the paper "Distributed Representations of Words and Phrases and their Compositionality," for small training datasets, the count of negative samples is taken between 5 and 20, and for large training datasets, it is recommended between 2 and 5.

Practically, negative samples are the inputs for which there should be no output determination, and just a vector with all 0s should be produced.

Note   A combination of subsampling and negative sampling reduces the training process load up to great extent.

The word2vec models have helped in achieving better quality of vector representations of words by making use of the combination of models on a collection of syntactic and semantic language tasks. With the advances in the computation resources, faster algorithms, and availability of textual data, it is possible to train high quality word vectors as compared to the earlier proposed neural network models.

In the next section we will be looking at the implementation of the skip-gram and CBOW models using TensorFlow. The credit to the structure of these goes to a combination of online courses and material available during the time of writing.

Word2vec Code

The TensorFlow library has made our lives easier by introducing multiple predefined functions to be used in the implementation of word2vec algorithms. This section includes the implementation for both the word2vec algos, skip-gram, and CBOW models.

The first part of the code at the start of this section is common for both the skip-gram and CBOW models, and it is later followed by the respective implementations in the skip-gram and CBOW code subsections.

Note   The data used for our exercise is a compressed format of the English Wikipedia dump made on March 3, 2006. It is available from the following link: http://mattmahoney.net/dc/textdata.html.

Import the required packages for the word2vec implementation as follows:

```
"""Importing the required packages"""
import random
import collections
import math
import os
import zipfile
import time
import re
import numpy as np
import tensorflow as tf

from matplotlib import pylab
%matplotlib inline

from six.moves import range
from six.moves.urllib.request import urlretrieve

"""Make sure the dataset link is copied correctly"""
dataset_link = 'http://mattmahoney.net/dc/'
zip_file = 'text8.zip'
```

The function data_download() downloads the cleaned up dataset of Wikipedia articles collected by Matt Mahoney and stores it as a separate file under the current working directory.

```python
def data_download(zip_file):
    """Downloading the required file"""
    if not os.path.exists(zip_file):
        zip_file, _ = urlretrieve(dataset_link + zip_file, zip_
        file)
        print('File downloaded successfully!')
    return None
data_download(zip_file)
```

```
> File downloaded successfully!
```

The zipped text dataset is extracted within an internal folder dataset and is used later to train the model.

```python
"""Extracting the dataset in separate folder"""

extracted_folder = 'dataset'

if not os.path.isdir(extracted_folder):
    with zipfile.ZipFile(zip_file) as zf:
        zf.extractall(extracted_folder)
with open('dataset/text8') as ft_ :
    full_text = ft_.read()
```

As the input data has multiple punctuation and other symbols across the text, the same are replaced with their respective tokens, with the type of punctuation and symbol name in the token. This helps the model to identify each of the punctuation and other symbols individually and produce a vector. The function text_processing() performs this operation. It takes the Wikipedia text data as input.

```python
def text_processing(ft8_text):
    """Replacing punctuation marks with tokens"""
    ft8_text = ft8_text.lower()
    ft8_text = ft8_text.replace('.', ' <period> ')
```

```
    ft8_text = ft8_text.replace(',', ' <comma> ')
    ft8_text = ft8_text.replace('"', ' <quotation> ')
    ft8_text = ft8_text.replace(';', ' <semicolon> ')
    ft8_text = ft8_text.replace('!', ' <exclamation> ')
    ft8_text = ft8_text.replace('?', ' <question> ')
    ft8_text = ft8_text.replace('(', ' <paren_l> ')
    ft8_text = ft8_text.replace(')', ' <paren_r> ')
    ft8_text = ft8_text.replace('--', ' <hyphen> ')
    ft8_text = ft8_text.replace(':', ' <colon> ')
    ft8_text_tokens = ft8_text.split()
    return ft8_text_tokens

ft_tokens = text_processing(full_text)
```

To improve the quality of the vector representations produced, it is recommended to remove the noise related to the words, i.e., words with a frequency of less than 7 in the input dataset, as these words will not have enough information to provide the context they are present in.

One can change this threshold by checking the distribution of the word count and in the dataset. For convenience, we have taken it as 7 here.

```
"""Shortlisting words with frequency more than 7"""
word_cnt = collections.Counter(ft_tokens)
shortlisted_words = [w for w in ft_tokens if word_cnt[w] > 7 ]
```

List the top words present in the dataset on the basis of their frequency, as follows:

```
print(shortlisted_words[:15])
```

```
> ['anarchism', 'originated', 'as', 'a', 'term', 'of', 'abuse',
'first', 'used', 'against', 'early', 'working', 'class',
'radicals', 'including']
```

Check the stats of the total words present in the dataset.

```
print("Total number of shortlisted words : ",len(shortlisted_
words))
print("Unique number of shortlisted words : ",len(set(shortlisted_
words)))
> Total number of shortlisted words :   16616688
> Unique number of shortlisted words :   53721
```

To process the unique words present in the corpus, we have made a set of the words, followed by their frequency in the training dataset. The following function creates a dictionary and converts words to integers and, conversely, integers to words. The most frequent word is assigned the least value, 0, and in similar fashion, numbers are assigned to other words. Conversion of words to integers has been stored in a separate list.

```
def dict_creation(shortlisted_words):
    """The function creates a dictionary of the words present
    in dataset along with their frequency order"""
    counts = collections.Counter(shortlisted_words)
    vocabulary = sorted(counts, key=counts.get, reverse=True)
    rev_dictionary_ = {ii: word for ii, word in
    enumerate(vocabulary)}
    dictionary_ = {word: ii for ii, word in rev_dictionary_.
    items()}
    return dictionary_, rev_dictionary_

dictionary_, rev_dictionary_ = dict_creation(shortlisted_words)
words_cnt = [dictionary_[word] for word in shortlisted_words]
```

The variables created up to this point are common and could be used in the implementation of the either of the word2vec models. The next subsections include the implementation of both architectures.

Skip-Gram Code

A subsampling approach has been coupled in the skip-gram model to deal with the stopwords in the text. All the words with higher frequency and without any significant context around the center words are removed by putting a threshold on their frequency. This results in faster training and better word vector representations.

Note   We have made use of the probability score function given in the paper on skip-gram for the implementation here. For each word, w_i, in the training set, we'll discard it with the probability given by

$$P\left(w_i\right) = 1 - \left(\sqrt{\frac{t}{f\left(w_i\right)}}\right)$$

where *t* is a threshold parameter and *f(w_i)* is the frequency of word w_i in the total dataset.

```
"""Creating the threshold and performing the subsampling"""
thresh = 0.00005
word_counts = collections.Counter(words_cnt)
total_count = len(words_cnt)
freqs = {word: count / total_count for word, count in word_
counts.items()}
p_drop = {word: 1 - np.sqrt(thresh/freqs[word]) for word in
word_counts}
train_words = [word for word in words_cnt if p_drop[word] <
random.random()]
```

As the skip-gram model takes the center word and predicts words surrounding it, the skipG_target_set_generation() function creates the input for the skip-gram model in the desired format:

```
def skipG_target_set_generation(batch_, batch_index, word_
window):
    """The function combines the words of given word_window
    size next to the index, for the SkipGram model"""
    random_num = np.random.randint(1, word_window+1)
    words_start = batch_index - random_num if (batch_index -
    random_num) > 0 else 0
    words_stop = batch_index + random_num
    window_target = set(batch_[words_start:batch_index] +
    batch_[batch_index+1:words_stop+1])
    return list(window_target)
```

The skipG_batch_creation() function makes use of the skipG_target_set_generation() function and creates a combined format of the center word and the words surrounding it on either side as target text and returns the batch output, as follows:

```
def skipG_batch_creation(short_words, batch_length, word_
window):
    """The function internally makes use of the skipG_target_
    set_generation() function and combines each of the label
    words in the shortlisted_words with the words of word_
    window size around"""
    batch_cnt = len(short_words)//batch_length
    short_words = short_words[:batch_cnt*batch_length]

    for word_index in range(0, len(short_words), batch_length):
        input_words, label_words = [], []
        word_batch = short_words[word_index:word_index+batch_
        length]
```

```
for index_ in range(len(word_batch)):
    batch_input = word_batch[index_]
    batch_label = skipG_target_set_generation(word_
    batch, index_, word_window)
    # Appending the label and inputs to the initial
    list. Replicating input to the size of labels in
    the window
    label_words.extend(batch_label)
    input_words.extend([batch_input]*len(batch_label))
    yield input_words, label_words
```

The following code registers a TensorFlow graph for use of the
skip-gram implementation, declaring the variable's inputs and labels
placeholders, which will be used to assign one-hot-encoded vectors for
input words and batches of varying size, as per the combination of the
center and surrounding words:

```
tf_graph = tf.Graph()
with tf_graph.as_default():
    input_ = tf.placeholder(tf.int32, [None], name='input_')
    label_ = tf.placeholder(tf.int32, [None, None],
    name='label_')
```

The code following declares variables for the embedding matrix, which
has a dimension equal to the size of the vocabulary and the dimension of
the word embedding vector:

```
with tf_graph.as_default():
    word_embed = tf.Variable(tf.random_uniform((len(rev_
    dictionary_), 300), -1, 1))
    embedding = tf.nn.embedding_lookup(word_embed, input_)
```

The `tf.train.AdamOptimizer` uses Diederik P. Kingma and Jimmy Ba's Adam algorithm (http://arxiv.org/pdf/1412.6980v8.pdf) to control the learning rate. For further information, refer additionally to the following paper by Bengio: http://arxiv.org/pdf/1206.5533.pdf.

```python
"""The code includes the following :
 # Initializing weights and bias to be used in the softmax layer
 # Loss function calculation using the Negative Sampling
 # Usage of Adam Optimizer
 # Negative sampling on 100 words, to be included in the loss
   function
 # 300 is the word embedding vector size
"""
vocabulary_size = len(rev_dictionary_)

with tf_graph.as_default():
    sf_weights = tf.Variable(tf.truncated_normal((vocabulary_
    size, 300), stddev=0.1) )
    sf_bias = tf.Variable(tf.zeros(vocabulary_size) )

    loss_fn = tf.nn.sampled_softmax_loss(weights=sf_weights,
                                        biases=sf_bias,
                                        labels=label_,
                                        inputs=embedding,
                                        num_sampled=100, num_
                                        classes=vocabulary_
                                        size)
    cost_fn = tf.reduce_mean(loss_fn)
    optim = tf.train.AdamOptimizer().minimize(cost_fn)
```

To ensure that the word vector representation is holding the semantic similarity among words, a validation set is generated in the following section of code. This will select a combination of common and uncommon words across the corpus and return the words closest to them on the basis of the cosine similarity between the word vectors.

```
"""The below code performs the following operations :
 # Performing validation here by making use of a random
   selection of 16 words from the dictionary of desired size
 # Selecting 8 words randomly from range of 1000
 # Using the cosine distance to calculate the similarity
 between the words
 """
with tf_graph.as_default():
    validation_cnt = 16
    validation_dict = 100

    validation_words = np.array(random.sample(range(validation_
    dict), validation_cnt//2))
    validation_words = np.append(validation_words, random.sample
    (range(1000,1000+validation_dict), validation_cnt//2))
    validation_data = tf.constant(validation_words, dtype=tf.
    int32)

    normalization_embed = word_embed / (tf.sqrt(tf.reduce_
    sum(tf.square(word_embed), 1, keep_dims=True)))
    validation_embed = tf.nn.embedding_lookup(normalization_
    embed, validation_data)
    word_similarity = tf.matmul(validation_embed,
    tf.transpose(normalization_embed))
```

Create a folder model_checkpoint in the current working directory to store the model checkpoints.

```
"""Creating the model checkpoint directory"""
!mkdir model_checkpoint

epochs = 2              # Increase it as per computation
                        resources. It has been kept low here
                        for users to replicate the process,
                        increase to 100 or more
batch_length = 1000
word_window = 10

with tf_graph.as_default():
    saver = tf.train.Saver()

with tf.Session(graph=tf_graph) as sess:
    iteration = 1
    loss = 0
    sess.run(tf.global_variables_initializer())

    for e in range(1, epochs+1):
        batches = skipG_batch_creation(train_words, batch_
        length, word_window)
        start = time.time()
        for x, y in batches:
            train_loss, _ = sess.run([cost_fn, optim],
                                    feed_dict={input_: x,
                                    label_: np.array(y)[:,
                                    None]})
            loss += train_loss

            if iteration % 100 == 0:
                end = time.time()
```

```python
        print("Epoch {}/{}".format(e, epochs), ",
        Iteration: {}".format(iteration),
            ", Avg. Training loss: {:.4f}".
            format(loss/100),", Processing : {:.4f}
            sec/batch".format((end-start)/100))
        loss = 0
        start = time.time()

    if iteration % 2000 == 0:
        similarity_ = word_similarity.eval()
        for i in range(validation_cnt):
            validated_words = rev_dictionary_
            [validation_words[i]]
            top_k = 8 # number of nearest neighbors
            nearest = (-similarity_[i, :]).argsort()
            [1:top_k+1]
            log = 'Nearest to %s:' % validated_words
            for k in range(top_k):
                close_word = rev_dictionary_
                [nearest[k]]
                log = '%s %s,' % (log, close_word)
            print(log)

        iteration += 1
    save_path = saver.save(sess, "model_checkpoint/skipGram_
    text8.ckpt")
    embed_mat = sess.run(normalization_embed)

> Epoch 1/2 , Iteration: 100 , Avg. Training loss: 6.1494 ,
Processing : 0.3485 sec/batch
> Epoch 1/2 , Iteration: 200 , Avg. Training loss: 6.1851 ,
Processing : 0.3507 sec/batch
> Epoch 1/2 , Iteration: 300 , Avg. Training loss: 6.0753 ,
Processing : 0.3502 sec/batch
```

```
> Epoch 1/2 , Iteration: 400 , Avg. Training loss: 6.0025 ,
Processing : 0.3535 sec/batch
> Epoch 1/2 , Iteration: 500 , Avg. Training loss: 5.9307 ,
Processing : 0.3547 sec/batch
> Epoch 1/2 , Iteration: 600 , Avg. Training loss: 5.9997 ,
Processing : 0.3509 sec/batch
> Epoch 1/2 , Iteration: 700 , Avg. Training loss: 5.8420 ,
Processing : 0.3537 sec/batch
> Epoch 1/2 , Iteration: 800 , Avg. Training loss: 5.7162 ,
Processing : 0.3542 sec/batch
> Epoch 1/2 , Iteration: 900 , Avg. Training loss: 5.6495 ,
Processing : 0.3511 sec/batch
> Epoch 1/2 , Iteration: 1000 , Avg. Training loss: 5.5558 ,
Processing : 0.3560 sec/batch
> .................
> Nearest to during: stress, shipping, bishoprics, accept,
produce, color, buckley, victor,
> Nearest to six: article, incorporated, raced, interval,
layouts, confused, spitz, masculinity,
> Nearest to all: cm, unprotected, fit, tom, opold, render,
perth, temptation,
> Nearest to th: ponder, orchids, shor, polluted, firefighting,
hammering, bonn, suited,
> Nearest to many: trenches, parentheses, essential, error,
chalmers, philo, win, mba,
> .................
```

A similar output will be printed for all other iterations, and the trained network will have been restored for further use.

```
"""The Saver class adds ops to save and restore variables to
and from checkpoints."""
with tf_graph.as_default():
    saver = tf.train.Saver()

with tf.Session(graph=tf_graph) as sess:
    """Restoring the trained network"""
    saver.restore(sess, tf.train.latest_checkpoint('model_
    checkpoint'))
    embed_mat = sess.run(word_embed)
> INFO:tensorflow:Restoring parameters from model_checkpoint/
skipGram_text8.ckpt
```

We have used the t-distributed stochastic neighbor embedding (t-SNE) for the purpose of visualization (https://lvdmaaten.github.io/tsne/). The high-dimensional, 300 vector representation of 250 random words has been used across a two-dimensional vector space. t-SNE ensures that the initial structure of the vector is reserved in the new dimension, even after conversion.

```
word_graph = 250
tsne = TSNE()
word_embedding_tsne = tsne.fit_transform(embed_mat[:word_graph, :])
```

As we can observe in Figure 2-13, words with semantic similarity have been placed closer to one another in their representation in the two-dimensional space, thereby retaining their similarity even after the dimensions have been further reduced. For example, words such as *year*, *years*, and *age* have been placed near one another and far from words

such as *international* and *religious*. The model can be trained for a higher
number of iterations, to achieve a better representation of the word
embeddings, and further changes can be made in the threshold values, to
fine-tune the results.

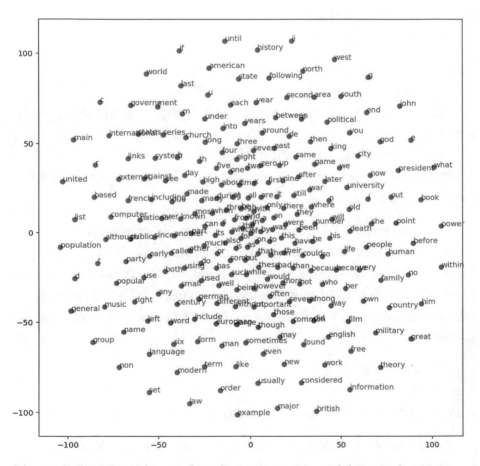

Figure 2-13. *Two-dimensional representation of the word vectors
obtained after training the Wikipedia corpus using a skip-gram model*

CBOW Code

The CBOW model considers the surrounding words and predicts the center word. Therefore, the batch and label generation have been achieved using the cbow_batch_creation() function, which assigns the target word in the label_ variable and the surrounding words in the context in the batch variable, when the desired word_window size is passed to the function.

```
data_index = 0

def cbow_batch_creation(batch_length, word_window):
    """The function creates a batch with the list of the label
    words and list of their corresponding words in the context of
    the label word."""
    global data_index
    """Pulling out the centered label word, and its next word_
    window count of surrounding words
    word_window : window of words on either side of the center
    word
    relevant_words : length of the total words to be picked in
    a single batch, including the center word and the word_
    window words on both sides
    Format :  [ word_window ... target ... word_window ] """
    relevant_words = 2 * word_window + 1

    batch = np.ndarray(shape=(batch_length,relevant_words-1),
    dtype=np.int32)
    label_ = np.ndarray(shape=(batch_length, 1), dtype=np.
    int32)

    buffer = collections.deque(maxlen=relevant_words)
    # Queue to add/pop
```

```
#Selecting the words of length 'relevant_words' from the
starting index
for _ in range(relevant_words):
    buffer.append(words_cnt[data_index])
    data_index = (data_index + 1) % len(words_cnt)

for i in range(batch_length):
    target = word_window  # Center word as the label
    target_to_avoid = [ word_window ] # Excluding the
    label, and selecting only the surrounding words

    # add selected target to avoid_list for next time
    col_idx = 0
    for j in range(relevant_words):
        if j==relevant_words//2:
            continue
        batch[i,col_idx] = buffer[j] # Iterating till the
        middle element for window_size length
        col_idx += 1
    label_[i, 0] = buffer[target]

    buffer.append(words_cnt[data_index])
    data_index = (data_index + 1) % len(words_cnt)

assert batch.shape[0]==batch_length and batch.shape[1]==
relevant_words-1
return batch, label_
```

Ensuring the cbow_batch_creation() function is working in accordance with the CBOW model input, a test sample of the first batch of label and words of window length 1 and 2 around it has been taken and the results are printed.

```
for num_skips, word_window in [(2, 1), (4, 2)]:
    data_index = 0
    batch, label_ = cbow_batch_creation(batch_length=8, word_
    window=word_window)
    print('\nwith num_skips = %d and word_window = %d:' % (num_
    skips, word_window))

    print('batch:', [[rev_dictionary_[bii] for bii in bi] for
    bi in batch])
    print('label_:', [rev_dictionary_[li] for li in label_.
    reshape(8)])
>>
> with num_skips = 2 and word_window = 1:
    batch: [['anarchism', 'as'], ['originated', 'a'], ['as',
    'term'], ['a', 'of'], ['term', 'abuse'], ['of', 'first'],
    ['abuse', 'used'], ['first', 'against']]
    label_: ['originated', 'as', 'a', 'term', 'of', 'abuse',
    'first', 'used']

> with num_skips = 4 and word_window = 2:
    batch: [['anarchism', 'originated', 'a', 'term'],
    ['originated', 'as', 'term', 'of'], ['as', 'a', 'of', 'abuse'],
    ['a', 'term', 'abuse', 'first'], ['term', 'of', 'first',
    'used'], ['of', 'abuse', 'used', 'against'], ['abuse', 'first',
    'against', 'early'], ['first', 'used', 'early', 'working']]
    label_: ['as', 'a', 'term', 'of', 'abuse', 'first', 'used',
    'against']
```

The following code declares the variables being used in the CBOW model configuration. The word-embedding vector has been assigned a size of 128, and on either side of the target word, 1 word has been taken into account for the prediction, as follows:

```
num_steps = 100001
"""Initializing :
   # 128 is the length of the batch considered for CBOW
   # 128 is the word embedding vector size
   # Considering 1 word on both sides of the center label words
   # Consider the center label word 2 times to create the
     batches
"""

batch_length = 128
embedding_size = 128
skip_window = 1
num_skips = 2
```

To register a TensorFlow graph for use of the CBOW implementation and to calculate the cosine similarity between the vectors produced, use the following code:

Note   This is a separate graph from the one used in the skip-gram code, so both the codes could be used in a single script.

```
"""The below code performs the following operations :
 # Performing validation here by making use of a random
   selection of 16 words from the dictionary of desired size
 # Selecting 8 words randomly from range of 1000
 # Using the cosine distance to calculate the similarity
   between the words
"""

tf_cbow_graph = tf.Graph()

with tf_cbow_graph.as_default():
    validation_cnt = 16
```

```
validation_dict = 100

validation_words = np.array(random.sample(range(validation_
dict), validation_cnt//2))
validation_words = np.append(validation_words,random.sample
(range(1000,1000+validation_dict), validation_cnt//2))

train_dataset = tf.placeholder(tf.int32, shape=[batch_
length,2*skip_window])
train_labels = tf.placeholder(tf.int32, shape=[batch_
length, 1])
validation_data = tf.constant(validation_words, dtype=tf.
int32)

"""
Embeddings for all the words present in the vocabulary
"""
with tf_cbow_graph.as_default() :
    vocabulary_size = len(rev_dictionary_)

    word_embed = tf.Variable(tf.random_uniform([vocabulary_
    size, embedding_size], -1.0, 1.0))

    # Averaging embeddings accross the full context into a
    single embedding layer
    context_embeddings = []
    for i in range(2*skip_window):
        context_embeddings.append(tf.nn.embedding_lookup(word_
        embed, train_dataset[:,i]))

    embedding =  tf.reduce_mean(tf.stack(axis=0,values=context_
    embeddings),0,keep_dims=False)
```

The following section of code computes the softmax loss using the negative sampling of 64 words and further optimizes the weights, biases, and word embeddings produced across the model training. The AdaGrad optimizer(www.jmlr.org/papers/volume12/duchi11a/duchi11a.pdf) has been used for this purpose.

```
"""The code includes the following :
 # Initializing weights and bias to be used in the softmax
   layer
 # Loss function calculation using the Negative Sampling
 # Usage of AdaGrad Optimizer
 # Negative sampling on 64 words, to be included in the loss
   function
"""
with tf_cbow_graph.as_default() :
    sf_weights = tf.Variable(tf.truncated_normal([vocabulary_
    size, embedding_size],
                     stddev=1.0 / math.sqrt(embedding_size)))
    sf_bias = tf.Variable(tf.zeros([vocabulary_size]))

    loss_fn = tf.nn.sampled_softmax_loss(weights=sf_weights,
    biases=sf_bias, inputs=embedding,
                     labels=train_labels, num_sampled=64,
                     num_classes=vocabulary_size)
    cost_fn = tf.reduce_mean(loss_fn)
    """Using AdaGrad as optimizer"""
    optim = tf.train.AdagradOptimizer(1.0).minimize(cost_fn)
```

Further, a cosine similarity is computed to ensure the closeness of the semantically similar words.

```
"""
Using the cosine distance to calculate the similarity between
the batches and embeddings of other words
"""
with tf_cbow_graph.as_default() :
    normalization_embed = word_embed / tf.sqrt(tf.reduce_
    sum(tf.square(word_embed), 1, keep_dims=True))
    validation_embed = tf.nn.embedding_lookup(normalization_
    embed, validation_data)
    word_similarity = tf.matmul(validation_embed,
    tf.transpose(normalization_embed))

with tf.Session(graph=tf_cbow_graph) as sess:
    sess.run(tf.global_variables_initializer())

    avg_loss = 0
    for step in range(num_steps):
        batch_words, batch_label_ = cbow_batch_creation(batch_
        length, skip_window)
        _, l = sess.run([optim, loss_fn], feed_dict={train_
        dataset : batch_words, train_labels : batch_label_ })
        avg_loss += l
        if step % 2000 == 0 :
            if step > 0 :
                avg_loss = avg_loss / 2000
            print('Average loss at step %d: %f' % (step,
            np.mean(avg_loss) ))
            avg_loss = 0

        if step % 10000 == 0:
            sim = word_similarity.eval()
```

```
        for i in range(validation_cnt):
            valid_word = rev_dictionary_[validation_
            words[i]]
            top_k = 8 # number of nearest neighbors
            nearest = (-sim[i, :]).argsort()[1:top_k+1]
            log = 'Nearest to %s:' % valid_word
            for k in range(top_k):
                close_word = rev_dictionary_[nearest[k]]
                log = '%s %s,' % (log, close_word)
            print(log)
    final_embeddings = normalization_embed.eval()
```

> Average loss at step 0: 7.807584
> Nearest to can: ambients, darpa, herculaneum, chocolate, alloted, bards, coyote, analogy,
> Nearest to or: state, stopping, falls, markus, bellarmine, bitrates, snub, headless,
> Nearest to will: cosmologies, valdemar, feeding, synergies, fence, helps, zadok, neoplatonist,
> Nearest to known: rationale, fibres, nino, logging, motherboards, richelieu, invaded, fulfill,
> Nearest to no: rook, logitech, landscaping, melee, eisenman, ecuadorian, warrior, napoli,
> Nearest to these: swinging, zwicker, crusader, acuff, ivb, karakoram, mtu, egg,
> Nearest to not: battled, grieg, denominators, kyi, paragliding, loxodonta, ceases, expose,
> Nearest to one: inconsistencies, dada, ih, gallup, ayya, float, subsumed, aires,
> Nearest to woman: philibert, lug, breakthroughs, ric, raman, uzziah, cops, chalk,

> Nearest to alternative: kendo, tux, girls, filmmakers, cortes, akio, length, grayson,
> Nearest to versions: helvetii, moody, denning, latvijas, subscripts, unamended, anodes, unaccustomed,
> Nearest to road: bataan, widget, commune, culpa, pear, petrov, accrued, kennel,
> Nearest to behind: coahuila, writeup, exarchate, trinidad, temptation, fatimid, jurisdictional, dismissed,
> Nearest to universe: geocentric, achieving, amhr, hierarchy, beings, diabetics, providers, persistent,
> Nearest to institute: cafe, explainable, approached, punishable, optimisation, audacity, equinoxes, excelling,
> Nearest to san: viscount, neum, sociobiology, axes, barrington, tartarus, contraband, breslau,
> Average loss at step 2000: 3.899086
> Average loss at step 4000: 3.560563
> Average loss at step 6000: 3.362137
> Average loss at step 8000: 3.333601
> .. ..

Using t-SNE for visualization purposes, the high-dimensional, 128, vector representation of 250 random words has been used to show the result across a two-dimensional space.

```
num_points = 250
tsne = TSNE(perplexity=30, n_components=2, init='pca',
n_iter=5000)
embeddings_2d = tsne.fit_transform(final_embeddings[1:num_
points+1, :])
```

The cbow_plot() function plots the dimensionally reduced vectors.

```
def cbow_plot(embeddings, labels):
    assert embeddings.shape[0] >= len(labels), 'More labels
    than embeddings'
    pylab.figure(figsize=(12,12))
    for i, label in enumerate(labels):
        x, y = embeddings[i,:]
        pylab.scatter(x, y)
        pylab.annotate(label, xy=(x, y), xytext=(5, 2),
        textcoords='offset points', ha='right', va='bottom')
    pylab.show()

words = [rev_dictionary_[i] for i in range(1, num_points+1)]
cbow_plot(embeddings_2d, words)
```

Figure 2-14 also illustrates that the words with semantic similarity are placed closer to one another in their two-dimensional space representation. For example, words like *right, left,* and *end* have been placed next to one another and far from such words as *one, two, three,* etc.

Among all the words presented here, we can observe, at the bottom left of the graph, that those related to a single alphabet are placed closer to one another. This helps us to understand how the model works and allocates the single characters with no significant meaning with similar word embeddings. The absence of such words as *a* and *i* in this cluster indicates that the word embeddings for the two alphabets related to these two words are not similar to other individual alphabets, as these hold actual meaning in the English language and are used more often than other alphabets, in which they are merely signs of a typo in the training dataset. A further training of the model with higher iterations can attempt to bring the vectors of these alphabets closer or further from the actual meaningful words of the language.

Note   Both CBOW and skip-gram methods use the local statistics to learn the word vector embeddings. Sometimes, better representations can be learned by exploring the global statistics of word pairs, and GloVe and FastText methodologies exploit this. One can refer to the following papers, respectively, for GloVe (`https://nlp.stanford.edu/pubs/ glove.pdf`) and FastText (`https://arxiv.org/pdf/1607.04606. pdf`) for further details on the algorithms concerned.

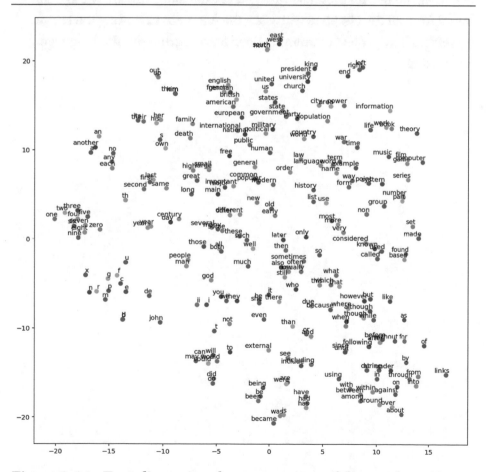

Figure 2-14.   *Two-dimensional representation of the word vectors obtained after training the Wikipedia corpus using the CBOW model*

Next Steps

This chapter introduced the word representation models used across research and industry domains. In addition to word2vec, one can also explore GloVe and FastText as other options for word embedding. We have tried to give a sample of one of the available approaches for word embeddings, using CBOW and skip-gram. In the next chapter, we will emphasize the different types of neural networks available, such as RNNs, LSTMs, Seq2Seq, along with their use cases for textual data. The knowledge combined from all the chapters will assist the reader in executing the entire pipeline of any project combining deep learning and natural language processing.

CHAPTER 3

Unfolding Recurrent Neural Networks

This chapter covers the use of contextual information across text. With textual work in any form, i.e., speech, text, and print, and in any language, to understand the information provided in it, we try to capture and relate the present and past contexts and aim to gain something meaningful from them. This is because the structure of text creates a link within a sentence and across sentences, just like thoughts, which are persistent throughout.

Traditional neural networks lack the ability to capture knowledge from previous events and pass it on to future events and related predictions. In this chapter, we will introduce a family of neural networks that can help us in persisting information over an extensive period.

In deep learning, all problems are generally classified into two types:

- **Fixed topological structure**: For images having static data, with use cases such as image classification

- **Sequential data**: For text/audio with dynamic data, in tasks related to text generation and voice recognition

Most problems with static data are solved using convolution neural networks (CNNs), and most problems related to sequential data are handled via recurrent neural networks (RNNs), particularly by long short-term memory (LSTM) methods. We will be going through both types of networks in detail throughout this chapter and cover use cases of the RNNs.

© Palash Goyal, Sumit Pandey, Karan Jain 2018
P. Goyal, et al., *Deep Learning for Natural Language Processing*,
https://doi.org/10.1007/978-1-4842-3685-7_3

In a normal feedforward network, the output to be classified at time t will not necessarily have any relation to the previous outputs that have been classified. In other words, the previously classified outputs don't play any role in the following classification problem.

But this is not practical, as there are few scenarios in which we must have the previous outputs to predict the new outputs. For example, while reading a book, we must know and remember the context mentioned in the chapters and what is being discussed throughout the book. Another major use case is sentiments analysis of a large portion of text. For all such problems RNNs have proven to be a very useful resource.

RNNs and LSTM networks have applications in diverse fields, including

- Chatbots

- Sequential pattern identification

- Image/handwriting detection

- Video and audio classification

- Sentiment analysis

- Time series modeling in finance

Recurrent Neural Networks

Recurrent neural networks are very effective and are able to perform computations of almost any type. RNNs have varied sets of use cases and can implement a set of multiple smaller programs, with each painting a separate picture on its own and all learning in parallel, to finally reveal the intricate effect of the collaboration of all such small programs.

RNNs are capable of performing such operations for two principal reasons:

- Hidden states being distributive by nature, store a lot of past information and pass it on efficiently.

- Hidden states are updated by nonlinear methods.

What Is Recurrence?

Recurrence is a recursive process in which a recurring function is called at each step to model the sets of temporal data.

What is a temporal data? Any unit of data that is dependent on the previous units of the data, particularly sequential data. For example, a company's share price is dependent on the prices of the share on previous days/weeks/months/years, hence, dependence on previous times or previous steps is important, thereby making such types of models extremely useful.

So, the next time you see any type of data having a temporal pattern, try using the types of models being discussed in the subsequent sections of this chapter, but be forewarned: have tons of data!

Differences Between Feedforward and Recurrent Neural Networks

In a normal feedforward network, data is fed to it discretely, without taking account of temporal relations. Such types of networks are useful for discrete prediction tasks, as the features aren't dependent on each other temporally. This represents the simplest form of neural network, with signals flowing in one direction, i.e., from input to output.

For example, if we took three months' stock price data and tried to predict the next month's price based on it, a feedforward network would take the data from the previous three months at once, as if there were no interdependence of data, which could turn out not to be the case.

However, a recurrent neural network would take the data for each month at a time, just like a time series model.

$$x(t) = x(t-1) + constant$$

A similar functionality of this concept drives RNNs to first perform some computation on the information of the past interval, say $t - 1$, and use it with the computation done on the present interval data, say t, and combine both to generate results for the next intervals.

A quick look at the differences between feedforward neural networks and RNNs reveals that the feedforward neural network takes decisions based only on the current input, and an RNN takes decisions based on the current and previous inputs and makes sure that the connections are built across the hidden layers as well.

Following are the main limitations of feedforward neural networks:

- Unsuitable for sequences, time series data, video streaming, stock data, etc.

- Do not bring memory factor in modeling

Figure 3-1 illustrates the differences between one type of RNN and a feedforward neural network.

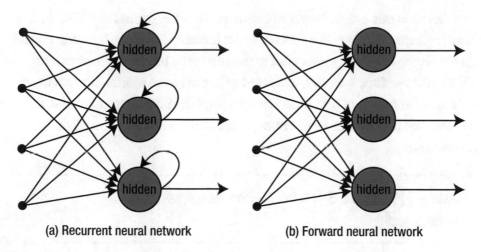

(a) Recurrent neural network   (b) Forward neural network

Figure 3-1. *Structural differentiation between a sample RNN and feedforward neural network*

Recurrent Neural Network Basics

We will quickly cover a thorough use case of RNNs before covering its basics and getting into its applications for NLP. Let's consider an example in which the RNN learns how a sum operator works and try to replicate it.

RNNs belong to family of algorithms with very powerful sequence modeling, and here we are going to see how, if given a sequence of binary inputs, the model is capable of adding the digits and providing us the summation as an output with almost perfect accuracy.

Given a binary string (a string with just 0s and 1s) of length 20, we must determine the count of 1s in a binary string. For example, "01010010011011100110" has 11 1s. So, the input for our program will be a string of length 20 that contains 0s and 1s, and the output must be a single number between 0 and 20 that represents the number of 1s in the string.

This task seems easy from a normal programming perspective, and the reader might think it similar to any typical "Hello World" problem. However, if we think of it from a machine's point of view, it is a model that can add numbers, a model that takes sequential binary inputs to give a summation. Well that's what we are dealing with!

Let's get our hands dirty and define certain key terms for RNNs. Before that, one thing to keep in mind while performing any deep learning model is the shape of a tensor being fed to the model as input. A tensor can be of any dimension, 3-D/4-D, when fed as input to the model. We can think of it as a list of lists of lists. This is a bit complex to understand at first, but we will see how to break this concept into further smaller and meaningful representations.

Note   [[[ ]]] is a 3-D tensor with three lists placed in hierarchically.

RNN requires a 3-D tensor as input, and it can be broken perfectly into the components shown in Figure 3-2.

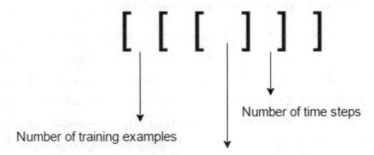

Figure 3-2. *Component-wise detail of a 3-D tensor used as input for RNN*

Note   There is no need to remember any of these, and as we go on looking at the structure of RNNs, you will understand the reasons behind considering the components in such a manner.

In the current problem, we are taking 20 time steps, or a sequence input of length 20, and each time step is being represented in 1-D, i.e., with a value of 0 or 1. The input time step can be in a different dimension, as per the problem at hand. Figure 3-3 shows the architecture of the model we will be using.

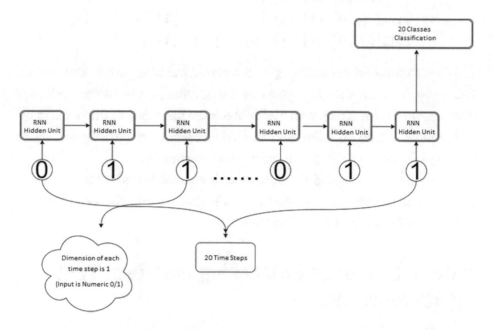

Figure 3-3. *RNN model architecture to compute the number of 1s in a 20 length sequence of binary digits*

In the model diagram, we can see that we have taken each of the binary units as an input at each of the time steps, i.e., 20 time steps, and passed them through a hidden layer, which is a recurrent layer in this case, and taken the output of the final layer to a normal classification multilayer perceptron.

Thus, the input to the TensorFlow's RNN is of the form

```
List =   [ [ [0] [1] [1] [1] [0] [0] [1] [1] [0] [1] [1] [1]
         [0] [0] [1] [1] [0] [1] [1] [1] ],
         [ [0] [1] [1] [1] [0] [0] [1] [1] [0] [1] [1] [1] [0]
         [0] [1] [1] [0] [1] [1] [1] ] ,
         ...., [ [0] [1] [1] [1] [0] [0] [1] [1] [0] [1] [1]
         [1] [0] [0] [1] [1] [0] [1] [1] [1] ]    ]
```

We recommend not focusing on the actual training part, because once you understand the data flow process, the training part becomes easier to understand, and you can train multiple related models. For once, don't shift your attention from the hidden RNN layers shown in the figure, and try to get the gist of the input being given to the model.

We will consider a slightly more complex example and try to use recurrent neural nets for sentiment classification (one of the most basic tasks in the field of NLP), as we go further.

Natural Language Processing and Recurrent Neural Networks

From the previous theories and explanations, one can easily guess that RNNs are tailor-made for sequential tasks, and what suits this problem statement more is *language*. From childhood, we humans have our brain specifically trained for proper structuring of any language. Let's assume English as being the most common language spoken across a major population. We know the prevalent structure of the language while we are talking and writing, because we have been taught it since childhood, and we are able to decipher it without any great effort.

We are supposed to make use of the proper language by using its *grammar*, which makes up the base rules of the language. Traditionally, NLP tasks are extremely difficult, because of the vastness of the grammar of different languages.

Hard-coding of the constraints with respect to each of the languages has its own drawbacks. No one wants to get in the weeds of hundreds and thousands of grammar rules present across diverse languages of world, and no one wants to learn or code it further, as per custom business requirements.

What saves us from all such hassles is deep learning, which targets the learning of the complex local structural formulation of all the languages and uses this learning to crack the complexities present in the problem set.

So, finally, we let our baby deep learning model, belonging to RNN category, learn on its own. We feed it the sequences of English sentences word-by-word and let it train on some supervised label, say, positive or negative for sentiment classification, or 1,2,3,4,5 for Star rating of text, for the time being.

Let's try to understand this by considering an example of the n-gram language model. Here, if we have four preceding words, 4-gram, our model has the capability to predict the most probable fifth word, by using the past information from the occurrences of such types of combinations of four words. Such types of models have direct use cases in problems such as Google Search for autocomplete suggestions.

Note   The actual models used for Google Search are not just direct implementations of any n-gram but a combination of much more complex models.

Let's try to understand this concept by considering a basic example. Suppose we have a normal sentence in English: "Sachin is a great cricketer." We can then represent this sentence in accordance with the input being taken by our deep learning model in the manner shown in Figure 3-4.

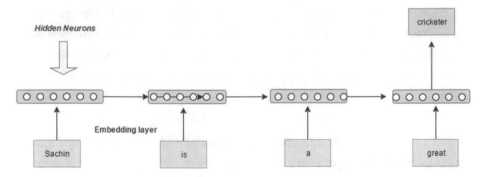

Figure 3-4. *Inputting the "Sachin is a great" sentence into the model*

Here, the last word, *cricketer*, can be judged from the sequence of previous four words *Sachin is a great*. We can judge that "Sachin is a great"—what? One answer could be "cricketer," as our thinking with respect to such a question and context has been modeled that way. Similarly, in some cases, we want the model to consider past historical events and make a prediction regarding future events. The events could be related to the information we are able to extract from the text as well.

A feedforward network takes the entire sentence as input at one go, whereas an RNN takes each of the words one by one and then aims to classify the given text. The preceding diagram would make it clearer.

The RNN takes the input in the form of the word embedding, which has been covered in Chapter 2, with two different types of models, CBOW and Skip-gram.

The word2vec models aim to initialize random vectors for each word, which are further learned to have meaningful vectors, to perform specific tasks. The word vectors can be formed of any given dimension and are able to encapsulate the information accordingly.

RNNs Mechanism

RNNs have creative applications in diverse fields, ranging from audio and text to images, including music generation, character generation, machine translation, etc. Let's try to understand the functional process of RNNs in a more beginner-friendly way and such that anyone with a non–deep learning background can understand it as well (Figure 3-5).

We are going to use the NumPy library for vector multiplications and depict the internal mathematics. This step function is recalled at each time step, i.e., recursion.

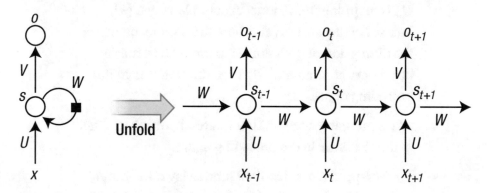

Figure 3-5. *Unrolled recurrent neural network*

First, defining the RNN class:

```
class RNN:
  # ...
  def step(self, x):

    # Update the Hidden state
    self.h = np.tanh(np.dot(self.W_hh, self.h) + np.dot
    (self.U_xh, x))

    # Compute the Output vector
    o = np.dot(self.V_hy, self.h)
    return o
```

The preceding pseudo code specifies the forward pass of a basic RNN. The function `step` is called at each time step of the RNN class. The parameters of this RNN are the three matrices (`W_hh, U_xh, V_hy`).

Following are the dimensions of each of the weight matrices from the preceding pseudo code and its equivalent entity from Figure 3-5:

- X_t is input at time step t.

- S_t is the hidden state at time step t. It's the "memory" of the network and is calculated based on the previous hidden state and the input at the current step.

- U_{xh} is mapping from input (x) to hidden layer (h), hence, $h \times$ dimension (x), where the dimension of x is the dimension of each time step input (1, in the case of a binary summation). Refer to the U matrix in the preceding figure.

- W_{hh} is mapping across hidden states, hence, $h \times h$. Refer to the W matrix in the preceding figure.

- V_{hy} is mapping from the final hidden layer to output y. Hence, h x dimension (y), where the dimension of y is the dimension of the output (20, in the case of the binary summation case considered previously). Refer to the V matrix in the preceding figure.

- o_t is the output at step t. For example, if we wanted to predict the next word in a sentence, it would be a vector of probabilities across our vocabulary.

The hidden state `self.h` is initialized with the zero vector. The `np.tanh` function implements a nonlinearity that squashes the activations to the range (-1, 1).

Notice briefly how this works. There are two terms inside of the `tanh` function: the first is based on the previous hidden state, and the second is based on the current input. In NumPy, `np.dot` performs the matrix multiplication.

The two intermediates interact with the addition and then get squashed into the new state vector by the `tanh` function. To infer the hidden state update in terms of mathematical notation, we can rewrite it as follows:

$$h_t = f_1\left(W_{hh} * h_{t-1} + U_{xh} * x_t\right)$$

where f_1 is generally taken as `tanh` or `sigmoid` and is applied element-wise.

We initialize the matrices of the RNN with random numbers, and the bulk of work performed during the training stage goes into the computation of the ideal matrices that give rise to the desirable behavior. This is measured with some loss function that expresses our preference for what kinds of outputs, o, we would like to see in response to our input sequences, x.

We can train an RNN model in multiple ways. However, agnostic to any specific way, RNNs have a very peculiar problem, and it is faced because, as the weights are propagated through time, they are multiplied recursively in the preceding functions, thereby giving rise to the following two types of scenarios:

- **Vanishing gradient**: If the weights are small, the subsequent values will keep on getting smaller and tend to ~0.

- **Exploding gradient**: If the weights are big, the final value will approach infinity.

Both of these problems make RNNs very sensitive to the number of time step or sequence limits. We can understand this in a detailed way by considering the output of the RNN. The output of an RNN network is represented as follows:

$$h_t = f_2\left(Ux_t + Vh_{t-1}\right)$$

where U and V are the weight matrices connecting the inputs and the recurrent outputs, respectively, and f_2 is *softmax* for classification tasks, and *L2 norm* (*squared error*) is for regression tasks. Softmax here is on the h_t outputs.

Note, however, that if we refer to, say, three time steps in our recurrent neural network (explained in the previous section), we have the following:

$$h_t = \sigma\left(Ux_t + V(\sigma\left(Ux_{t-1} + V(\sigma\left(Ux_{t-2}\right)\right)\right))\right)$$

From the preceding equation, we can infer, as the network grows deeper by the addition of more complex layers, and with propagation over time, that it will lead to gradient vanishing or exploding problems.

The gradient problem with the `sigmoid` function occurs when the input values are such that the output is close to either 0 or 1. At this point, the gradient is very small and tends to vanish, as shown in Figure 3-6.

1.0
0.8
0.6
0.4
0.2
0.0
y
−4
−2
0
2
4
x
f(x)
f'(x)

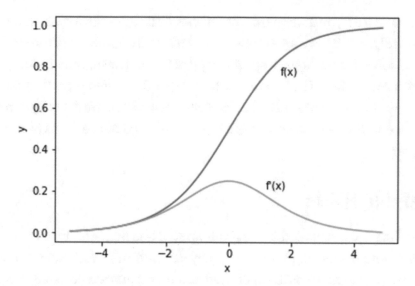

***Figure 3-6.** Logistic curve, at top, along with its first degree differentiation, below*

Figure 3-7 illustrates the vanishing gradient problem in a RNN.

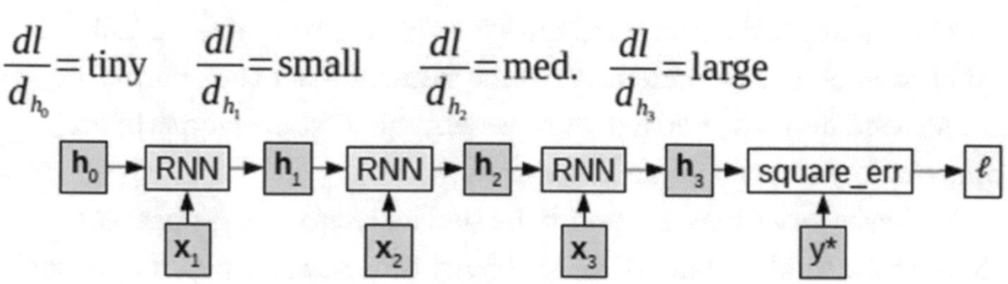

$\frac{dl}{d_{h_0}}$=tiny
$\frac{dl}{d_{h_1}}$=small
$\frac{dl}{d_{h_2}}$=med.
$\frac{dl}{d_{h_3}}$=large
h_0
RNN
h_1
RNN
h_2
RNN
h_3
square_err
ℓ
x_1
x_2
x_3
y*

***Figure 3-7.** Example of vanishing gradient*

As shown in the preceding figure (h_0, h_1, h_2, and h_3, are hidden states), at each time step, when we run the backpropagation algorithm, the gradient gets smaller and smaller, and by the time we get back to the beginning of the sentence, we have a gradient so small that it effectively has no capability to have a significant effect on the parameters that must be updated. The reason why this effect occurs is because unless $d\,h_{t-1}/d\,h_t$ is exactly 1, or $d\,h_{t-1}/d\,h_t = 1$, it will tend to either diminish or amplify the gradient $d\,l/d\,h_t$, and when this diminishes or its amplification is done repeatedly, it will have an exponential effect on the gradient of the loss.

To solve this problem, a specific type of hidden layer, called a long short-term memory (LSTM) network, and gated rectified units (GRUs) are used. The latter are special gated cells designed to intrinsically handle such scenarios. We will go through these briefly in later sections of this chapter.

Training RNNs

One of the most remarkable things about RNNs is their ability to be so flexible with respect to training that they can perform excellently on a wide range of problems, in both supervised and unsupervised domains. Before proceeding to the main topic, let's learn the deep secret about the hidden states (LSTM/GRU/sigmoidal neurons).

A curious mind might wonder exactly what a hidden state is. Is it like a normal feedforward network? Or is it even more complex in nature?

The answer to the preceding questions is that the mathematical representation of any hidden state is the same as that of any normal feedforward network, and it does represent the hidden features of the input, for any static/stateless dimension.

However, as we have seen with the special *recurrence* property of RNNs, in the hidden states of RNNs for any time interval step, it represents a contextual representation of all the previous time steps in a compressed dense manner. It holds, too, the semantic sequential information in the dense vector.

For example, the hidden state at time t, $H(t)$, contains some noisy and some true information of the time intervals $X(t-1), X(t-2), \ldots, X(0)$.

Considering the RNN training, for any problem with supervised learning, we must find a Loss function that helps in the update of weights that were initialized randomly, either through backpropagation or gradient descent.

Note   Readers unfamiliar with backpropagation implementation shouldn't be too worried, as modern libraries like TensorFlow and PyTorch have super-fast auto-differentiation processes that make such tasks much easier. One need only define the network architecture and targets. However, readers are advised to go through the backpropagation technique thoroughly, to experiment more with neural networks, as this serves as the backbone of any neural network training.

Now, let's create our initial example of binary sequence summation. Following is an explanation, in a step-by-step manner, of how the network functions and trains:

1.   Initialize the hidden states to a random number vector (size of the hidden layer is the free parameter that we set).

2.   Feed the binary number, 0 or 1, at each sequence step. Hence, calculating and updating the hidden vector at each step according to the following equation:

$$H(t) = tanh\big(U \cdot X(t) + V \cdot H(t-1)\big)$$

where, "." represents the dot product between the two matrices, and H, X, U, V have the same references as before.

3.   The last hidden layer (specifically in this case) is taken as output and fed into another multilayer perceptron (feedforward network).

So, basically, the last layer is a representation of the entire sequence, and this last layer (hidden representation at time t) is the most important layer. However, other hidden states at earlier time intervals $\{t\text{-}1, t\text{-}2,..., 0\}$ can also be utilized for other purposes.

Note   Unlike with traditional backpropagation, RNNs have a specific algorithm called backpropagation through time (BPTT). In BPTT, the gradient update for a layer at time t, is dependent on time $t\text{-}1, t\text{-}2,...,0$. So, in all its forms, backpropagation is done through sequential time steps. However, if one understands BPTT, it becomes apparent that it is just a special case of normal backpropagation.

Apart from training by taking the output from the last hidden layer, if one has a curious/intuitive mind, he/she may have wondered why we have not taken all the hidden states and averaged them out. Indeed, that's another means. If the reader has already concluded that, then it's good to know he/she is getting a good grasp on RNNs! Figure 3-8 displays multiple ways of utilizing the model output(s).

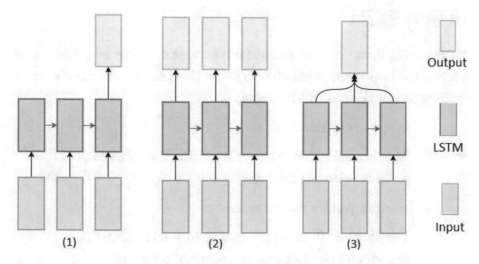

Figure 3-8. *An RNN can be trained in multiple ways, as required. One can take output of just the last time step, or all the time steps, or take the average of all the time steps.*

Meta Meaning of Hidden State of RNN

The hidden states in an RNN have immense importance. Apart from being the mathematical output of matrix multiplications, RNN hidden states hold some critical information about the data, i.e., particularly sequential information. The last hidden states of an RNN are capable of a wide variety of highly creative tasks. For example, there is a remarkably intuitive model called sequence-to-sequence (seq-to-seq or seq2seq) models. These models are used for machine translation, image captioning, etc. We will give a brief overview of how it works in the next sections, but coding and other details related to it is beyond the scope of this book.

Let's say we have a sentence in English, and we want to automatically convert/translate it into French using a seq2seq model. Intuitively, we feed the RNN model with a sequence of words, an English sentence, and consider only the last hidden output. This hidden output seems to store the most relevant information of the sentence. Next, we use this hidden state to initialize another RNN that will do the conversion. So simple, right?

Tuning RNNs

RNNs are highly critical to input variables and are very receptive in nature. A few of the important parameters in RNNs that play a major role in the training process include the following:

- Number of hidden layers

- Number of hidden units per layer (usually chosen as same number in each layer)

- Learning rate of the optimizer

- Dropout rate (initially successful dropout in RNNs is applied to feedforward connections only, not to recurrent ones)

- Number of iterations

Generally, we can plot the output with validation curves and learning curves and check for overfitting and underfitting. Training and testing the error at each split should be plotted, and according to the problem we check, if it is an overfit, then we can decrease the number of hidden layers, or hidden neurons, or add dropout, or increase the dropout rate, and vice versa.

However, apart from these considerations, the other major problem is with weights, for which we have weight/gradient clipping and multiple initialization functions in the TensorFlow library.

Long Short-Term Memory Networks

LSTM networks were first introduced by Sepp Hochreiter and Jürgen Schmidhuber in 1997 and solved the problem of retaining information for RNNs over longer time periods (`www.bioinf.jku.at/publications/older/2604.pdf`).

RNNs have proven to be the only choice for dealing with problems related to sequence classification, and they have proven to be appropriate to retain the information from the previous input data and to use that information to modify the output at any time step. However, if the length of the sequence is long enough, then the gradients computed during the training process of the RNN model, specifically backpropagation, either vanishes, owing to the cumulative multiplication effect of values between 0 and 1, or explodes, again owing to the cumulative multiplication of large values, thereby causing the model to train in a relatively slow manner.

A LSTM network is the savior here. It is the type of RNN architecture that helps in training the model over lengthy sequences and in the retention of the memory from previous time steps of input fed to the model. Ideally, it solves the gradient vanishing or gradient explosion problem, by introducing additional gates, input and forget gates, which allow for a better control over the gradient, by enabling what information to preserve and what to forget, thus controlling the access of the information to the present cell's state, which enables better preservation of "long-range dependencies."

Even though we could try other activation functions, such as ReLU, to reduce the problem, they would not solve the problem completely. This drawback of RNN led to the rise in the use of LSTM networks to effectively resolve the issue.

Components of LSTM

LSTM networks also have a chainlike structure, but the repeating module has a different structure. Instead of having a single neural network layer, there are four, interacting in a very special way. The structure of an LSTM cell is shown in Figure 3-9.

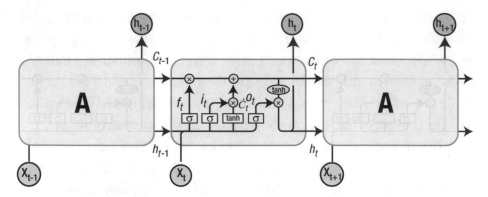

Figure 3-9. *LSTM module with four interacting layers*

LSTM is formed using multiple *gates*, which serve as a good option for regulating the information passing through. They have a sigmoid neural net layer, with output in [0,1] to weigh the passing limit of the component, and a point-wise multiplication operation.

In the preceding figure, C_i is the cell state, which is present across all the time steps and is changed by the interactions at each of the time steps. To retain the information flowing across an LSTM via the cell state, it has three types of gates:

- **Input gate**: To control the contribution from a new input to the memory

$$i_t = \sigma\left(W_i \cdot \left[h_{t-1}, x_t\right] + b_i\right)$$

$$\acute{C}_t = tanh\left(W_C \cdot \left[h_{t-1}, x_t\right] + b_c\right)$$

Here x_t denotes the input at time step t, h_{t-1} denotes the hidden state at time step t-1, i_t denotes the input gate layer output at time step t, $\acute{C}_t$ refers to candidate values to be added to input gate output at time step t, b_i and b_c denote the bias for the input gate layer and the candidate value computation, W_i and W_c denote the weights for the input gate layer and the candidate value computation.

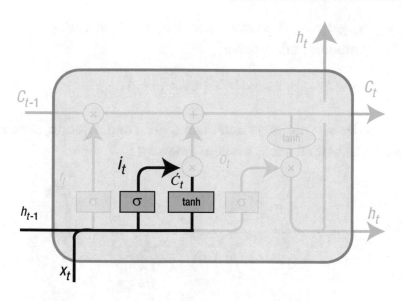

$$C_t = f_t * C_{t-1} + i_t * \acute{C}_t$$

Here, C_i denotes the cell state after time step i, and f_t denotes the forget state at time step t.

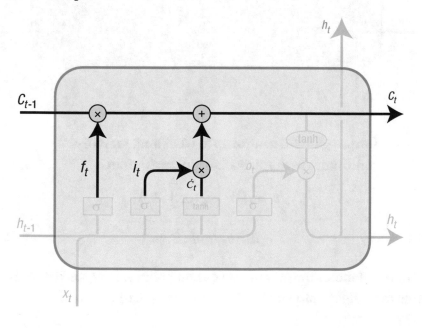

- **Forget gate**: To control the limit up to which a value is pertained in the memory

$$f_t = \sigma\left(W_f \cdot \left[h_{t-1}, x_t\right] + b_f\right)$$

Here, f_t denotes the forget state at time step t and, W_f and b_f denote the weights and bias for the forget state at time step t.

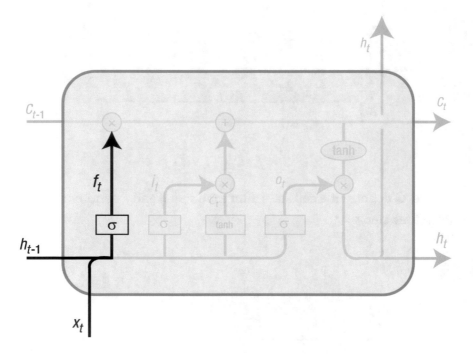

- **Output gate**: To control up to what limit memory contributes in the activation block of output

$$o_t = \sigma\left(W_o \cdot \left[h_{t-1}, x_t\right] + b_o\right)$$

$$h_t = o_t * tanh\left(C_t\right)$$

Here, o_t denotes the output gate output at time step t, and W_o and b_o denote the weights and bias for the output gate at time step t.

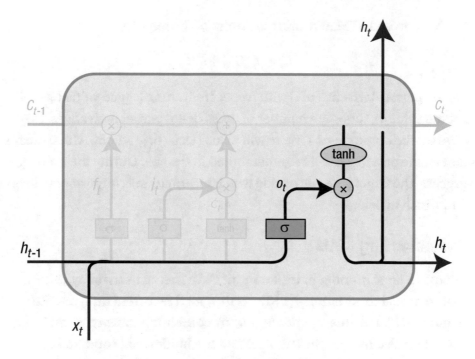

Today, LSTM networks have become a more popular choice than basic RNNs, as they have proven to work tremendously on diverse sets of problems. Most remarkable results are achieved with LSTM networks than RNNs, and now the phenomenon has extended such that wherever an RNN is quoted, it usually refers to LSTM network only.

How LSTM Helps to Reduce the Vanishing Gradient Problem

As we have mentioned previously, in a basic RNN, a vanishing gradient occurs during backpropagation, i.e., while calculating the gradient to update the weights, because it involves cascading of partial derivatives, and each of the partial derivatives involves a σ term, i.e., a sigmoid neural net layer. As the value of each of the sigmoid derivatives might become less than 1, thereby making the overall gradient values small enough that they won't be able to further update the weights, that means the model will stop learning!

Now, in an LSTM network, the output of the forget gate is

$$C_t = f_t {}^* C_{t-1} + i_t {}^* \acute{C}_t$$

So, the partial derivative of C with respect to its time lagged value C_{t-1} will get the value $f_t{}^\circ$, times the number of times of the partial derivatives. Now, if we set the output of $f = 1$, there will be no decay of gradient, which means that all the past input will be remembered in the cell. During the training process, the forget gate will decide which information is important to keep and which to delete.

Understanding GRUs

There is a large number of variations of LSTM being used today. One such reasonable variation of LSTM is the gated recurrent unit, or GRU (Figure 3-10). It forms an *update gate*, by combining the forget and input gates, and also merges the cell state and the hidden state and makes changes in the way the output is generated. The resulting models usually have lesser complexity, compared to the standard LSTM models.

A GRU controls the flow of information like an LSTM unit but without having to use a *memory unit*. It just exposes the full hidden content without any control.

It has been observed that LSTM works better for bigger datasets, while GRU works better for smaller datasets. As such, there is no hard and fast rule, as, to some extent, efficiency depends on the data and model complexity as well.

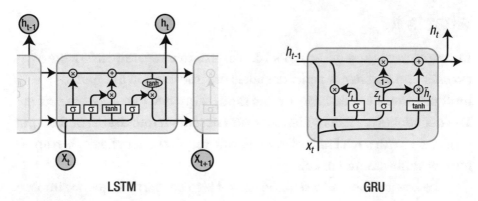

Figure 3-10. LSTM and GRU

Limitations of LSTMs

Apart from the complexity of LSTM networks, they are usually slower than other typical models. With careful initialization and training, even an RNN can deliver results similar to those of LSTM, and, too, with less computational complexity. Also, when recent information holds more importance than older information, there is no doubt that the LSTM model is always a better choice, but there are problems that we want to go further into the past to resolve. In such cases, a new mechanism, called the *attention* mechanism—which is a slightly modified version—is growing in popularity. We will cover it in a later subsection, "Attention Scoring."

Sequence-to-Sequence Models

Sequence-to-sequence (seq2seq) models are used for everything from chatbots to speech-to-text to dialog systems to QnA to image captioning. The key thing with seq2seq models is that the sequences preserve the order of the inputs, which is not the case with basic neural nets. There's certainly no good way to represent the concept of time and of things changing over time, so the seq2seq models allow us to process information that has a time, or an order of time, element attached to it. They allow us to preserve information that couldn't be by a normal neural network.

What Is It?

In simple terms, a seq2seq model consists of two separate RNNs, the *encoder* and *decoder*. An encoder takes the information as input in multiple time steps and *encodes* the input sequence into a *context vector*. The decoder takes that hidden state and *decodes* it into the desired output sequence. With such kinds of models, one requires a lot of data, like an unbelievable amount of data.

The key task behind a seq2seq model is to convert a sequence into a fixed size feature vector that encodes only the important information in the sequence, while losing the unnecessary information.

Let's consider the example of a basic question-and-answer system, in which the question is "How are you?" In this case, the model takes the sequence of words as input, so we are going to try to get each word in the sequence into a fixed-size feature vector that can then be used to predict the output, by model, for a structure answer. The model must remember the important things in the first sequence and also lose any unnecessary information in that sequence, to produce the relevant answers.

Figure 3-11 shows the unrolled version of encoder and decoder, for a better understanding of the whole process.

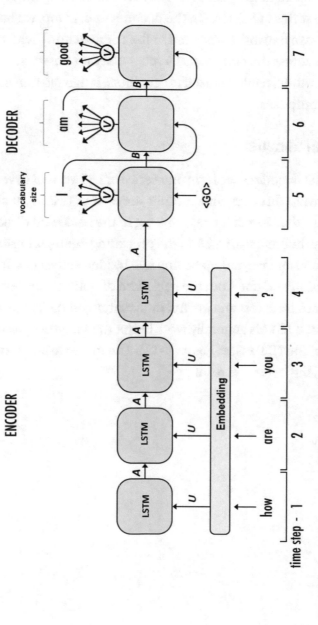

Figure 3-11. *Sample seq2seq model with input and output sentence*

In the encoder stage, we are feeding the network with the embedded word vector present in the question "How are you?", along with a set of weights to the series of LSTMs. On the decoder end, at top, we have a time-distributed dense network (explained in the code section), which is used to predict words across the current text's vocabulary for answers.

The same model could be used for chatbots, language translation, and other related purposes.

Bidirectional Encoder

In bidirectional encoders, we have one series of LSTMs that covers the text in the forward direction and another series of LSTMs, right above the previous series, that covers the text coming in the backward direction. So, the weights in this case, i.e., A in the preceding figure, is basically the hidden state, and we end up having two hidden states: one from the forward direction and one from the backward direction. This allows the network to learn from text and get full information on the context.

Bidirectional LSTMs generally work better than anything else for almost each of the NLP tasks (Figure 3-12). The more we add bidirectional LSTMs layers, the better the result.

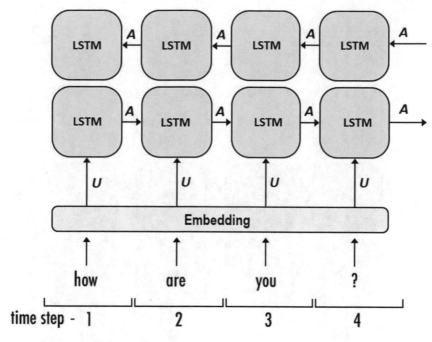

Figure 3-12. *Bidirectional encoder*

Stacked Bidirectional Encoder

For stacked bidirectional encoders, such as in the following figure, we have two bidirectional LSTMs or four layers. (One can go up to six bidirectional LSTMs, for more complex structures and to achieve better results.)

Each of these LSTM layers has weights inside, which are learning on their own and simultaneously influencing the weights in the preceding layers as well.

As the network moves forward in time, with respect to given input, and encounters new information from incoming text, it produces a hidden state representing everything useful present in the overall text (Figure 3-13).

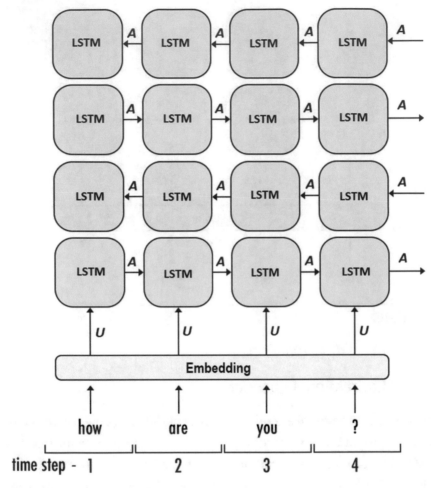

Figure 3-13. *Stacked bidirectional encoder*

Decoder

The encoder outputs the context vector, which offers a snapshot of the entire sequence occurring before. The context vector is used to predict the output, by passing it to the decoder.

In the decoder, we have a dense layer with softmax, just as in a normal neural network, and it is time-distributed, which means that we have one of these for each time step.

In Figure 3-14, the circles at the top represent the entire vocabulary, and the one with highest score corresponds to the output of that time step. This is valid, if we are working with text and are trying to get back the results in words only, and the top layer will have one neuron for every single word in the vocabulary. The top layer could often get super big with the increase in size of the vocabulary.

The important thing is that to start the prediction, we pass in a <GO> token to initiate the prediction process. What follows next is that we feed the <GO> token itself as the input on the first cell, and it now makes the prediction for the first word of our answer, along with the information from the context vector, following which we take the predicted first word from the model and feed that into the next time step as input, to get the second word prediction, and so on. This will lead to the creation of the whole text for our answer. Theoretically, in an ideal scenario, when predictions are right, the model should predict whatever we are trying to answer or translate.

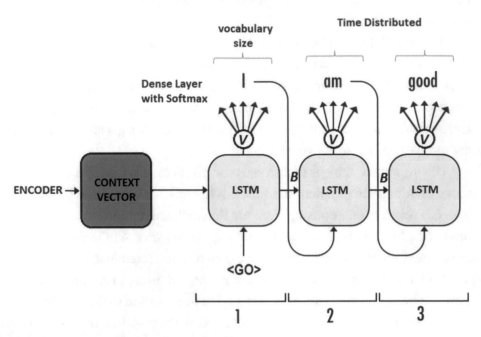

Figure 3-14. *Decoder*

Advanced Sequence-to-Sequence Models

Basic seq2seq models work well for normal tasks on short sentences, but they start to break on long sentences. Moreover, normal LSTMs can remember about 30 time steps and start to drop off very quickly after 30 time steps. If they're not trained enough, they drop off even sooner.

As compared to the basic seq2seq models, attention mechanisms perform better on the short-term length sequences. Moreover, using attention mechanisms, we can reach a maximum length of about 50 time steps. It is one of the major limitations in NLP currently that we don't have anything that can really go back in time and remember even a few paragraphs, let alone a whole book.

There are a few tricks to get around this. For example, we can flip the input and train the model backward, i.e., backward going in and forward coming out. This will often put the end words closer together and help in relating the predicting words better.

Sequence-to-sequences can be RNNs, LSTMs (preferred), or GRUs, and for lower-level tasks, bidirectional LSTMs are preferred. We will look at a few of the advanced models that are used to handle such issues.

Attention Scoring

Attention models look at the whole content shown and work out ways to figure out which word is most important for each of the words in the text. So, it sort of gives a score to every word in your sentence, and with that, it is able to get a sense that there are certain words that rely on some words a lot more than other ones.

The previous ways of text generation involved generating sentences very good at grammar, but that either got the names wrong or repeated some characters, such as a question mark. The best way to understand attention models is to think of them as kind of a little memory module that basically sits above the network and then looks at the words and picks the ones that are most important. For example, in the following sentence, clearly not all words are of equal importance:

Last month everyone went to the club, but I stayed at home.
Last month everyone went to the *club*, but *I stayed* at home.

The italic words in the second sentence are the ones that are noted and scored higher, compared to other words in the sentence. This helps in translation to different languages and for retaining context information as well, such as the event happened "last month," as this time information is required while doing the NLP tasks.

Adding attention helps in getting a fixed length vector, with a score attributed to each of the words telling us how important each of the words and the time steps are in the given sequence. This becomes important while doing translation. As when manual translation is done for a long sentence, we focus more on the particular words or phrases, irrespective of their position in the sentence. Attention helps in re-creating the same mechanism for neural networks.

As mentioned earlier, normal models fail to capture the crux of the full sentence, using a single hidden state only, which gets worse as the length increases. An attention vector (shown in Figure 3-15) helps in increasing the model's performance, by capturing the information from the overall input sentence at each of the steps of the decoder. This step makes sure that the decoder is not dependent only on the last decoder state but also on the combined weights of all the input states.

The best technique is to use bidirectional LSTMs, along with attention on top of it, in the encoder.

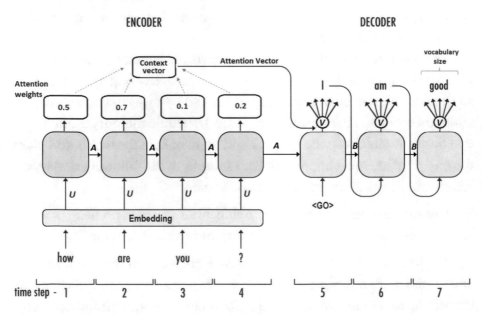

Figure 3-15. *Attention scoring network*

Figure 3-16 illustrates one such use case of an attention scoring network for language translation. The encoder takes the input tokens until it gets a special end token, say <DONE>, and then the decoder takes over and starts generating tokens, also finishing with its own end token of <DONE>.

The encoder changes its internal state as the English sentence tokens come in, and then, once the last token arrives, a final encoder state is taken and passed into the decoder, unchanged and repeatedly. In the decoder, every single German token is generated. The decoder also has its own dynamic internal state.

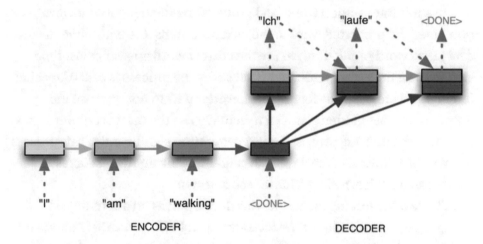

Figure 3-16. *Language translation using an attention scoring network*

Teacher Forcing

Teacher forcing uses the ground truth as input for each of the consecutive time steps, in lieu of the output of the network.

One can refer to the abstract of the original paper on teacher forcing, "Professor Forcing: A New Algorithm for Training Recurrent Networks," for a cogent explanation of the technique (https://papers.nips.cc/paper/6099-professor-forcing-a-new-algorithm-for-training-recurrent-networks.pdf).

> *The Teacher Forcing algorithm trains recurrent networks by supplying observed sequence values as inputs during training and using the network's own one-step-ahead predictions to do multi-step sampling. We introduce the Professor Forcing algorithm, which uses adversarial domain adaptation to encour-*

155

age the dynamics of the recurrent network to be the same when training the network and when sampling from the network over multiple time steps.

To understand this better, as we train the teacher forcing model, while doing the prediction part, we check whether every word predicted is right and use this information while backpropagating the network. However, we don't feed the predicted word to the next time steps. Instead, while making every next word prediction, we use the correct word answer of last time step for next time step prediction. That's why the process is called "teacher forcing." We are basically forcing the decoder part to not only use the output of the last hidden state but to actually use the correct answers. This improves the training process for text generation significantly. This process is not to be followed while doing the actual scoring on the test dataset. Make use of the learned weights for scoring step.

The teacher forcing technique was developed as an alternative to backpropagation-through-time for training an RNN. Figure 3-17 shows one such example of training an RNN using the teacher forcing mechanism.

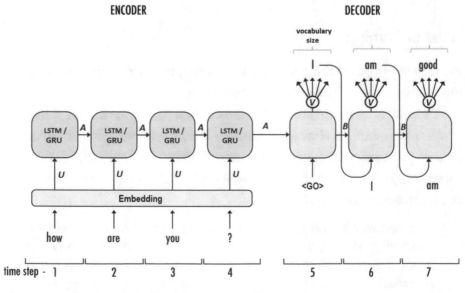

Figure 3-17. *Teacher forcing approach*

Peeking

Peeking involves feeding of the hidden state of the context vector straight through every step of the RNN or LSTM. The hidden state changes every time it goes through weights, and we make use of this updated hidden state and also keep the original context vector from the encoder, so that it checks the regular updates occurring, to figure out the way to better accuracy.

Peeking was proposed by Yoshua Bengio and others in the research paper "Learning Phrase Representations using RNN Encoder–Decoder for Statistical Machine Translation" (https://arxiv.org/abs/1406.1078).

> *We propose a novel neural network model called RNN Encoder–Decoder that consists of two RNNs. One RNN encodes a sequence of symbols into a fixed-length vector representation, and the other decodes the representation into another sequence of symbols. The encoder and decoder of the proposed model are jointly trained to maximize the conditional probability of a target sequence given a source sequence. The proposed model learns a semantically and syntactically meaningful representation of linguistic phrases.*

Sequence-to-Sequence Use Case

For the use case of seq2seq models, we have taken textual content of annotated corpus used in the research paper "Development of a benchmark corpus to support the automatic extraction of drug-related adverse effects from medical case reports" (www.sciencedirect.com/science/article/pii/S1532046412000615), by H. Gurulingappa.

> *The work presented here aims at generating a systematically annotated corpus that can support the development and validation of methods for the automatic extraction of drug-related adverse effects from medical case reports. The documents are*

systematically double annotated in various rounds to ensure consistent annotations. The annotated documents are finally harmonized to generate representative consensus annotations.

We have used an open source skip-gram model provided by NLPLab (http://evexdb.org/pmresources/vec-space-models/wikipedia-pubmed-and-PMC-w2v.bin), which was trained on all the PubMed abstracts and PMC full texts (4.08 million distinct words). The output of skip-gram model is a set of word vectors of 200 dimensions.

As usual import all the necessary modules first:

```
# Importing the required packages
import os
import re
import csv
import codecs
import numpy as np
import pandas as pd

import nltk
from nltk.corpus import stopwords
from nltk.stem import SnowballStemmer
from string import punctuation
from gensim.models import KeyedVectors
```

Check the Keras and TensorFlow version used for this exercise:

```
import keras
print(keras.__version__)
> 2.1.2
import tensorflow
print(tensorflow.__version__)
> 1.3.0
```

Make sure you have downloaded and saved the word embedding file from the previously mentioned link in your current working directory.

```
EMBEDDING_FILE = 'wikipedia-pubmed-and-PMC-w2v.bin'
print('Indexing word vectors')
> Indexing word vectors

word2vec = KeyedVectors.load_word2vec_format(EMBEDDING_FILE,
binary=True)
print('Found %s word vectors of word2vec' % len(word2vec.
vocab))
> Found 5443656 word vectors of word2vec

import copy
from keras.preprocessing.sequence import pad_sequences
> Using TensorFlow backend.
```

The ADE corpus used from the paper by Gurulingappa is distributed with three files: DRUG-AE.rel, DRUG-DOSE.rel, and ADE-NEG.txt. We are making use of the DRUG-AE.rel file, which provides relationships between drugs and adverse effects.

Following is a sample of the text from the file:

```
10030778 | Intravenous azithromycin-induced ototoxicity.
| ototoxicity | 43 | 54 | azithromycin | 22 | 34

10048291 | Immobilization, while Paget's bone disease was
present, and perhaps enhanced activation of dihydrotachysterol
by rifampicin, could have led to increased calcium-release into
the circulation. | increased calcium-release | 960 | 985 |
dihydrotachysterol | 908 | 926

10048291 | Unaccountable severe hypercalcemia in a patient
treated for hypoparathyroidism with dihydrotachysterol. |
hypercalcemia | 31 | 44 | dihydrotachysterol | 94 | 112
```

```
10082597 | METHODS: We report two cases of pseudoporphyria
caused by naproxen and oxaprozin. | pseudoporphyria | 620 | 635
| naproxen | 646 | 654
```

```
10082597 | METHODS: We report two cases of pseudoporphyria
caused by naproxen and oxaprozin. | pseudoporphyria | 620 | 635
| oxaprozin | 659 | 668
```

The format of the DRUG-AE.rel file is as follows, fields are separated by pipe delimiters:

Column-1: PubMed-ID

Column-2: Sentence

Column-3: Adverse-Effect

Column-4: Begin offset of Adverse-Effect at 'document level'

Column-5: End offset of Adverse-Effect at 'document level'

Column-6: Drug

Column-7: Begin offset of Drug at 'document level'

Column-8: End offset of Drug at 'document level'

Note   During annotation, documents were used in the following format: PubMed-ID \n \n Title \n \n Abstract.

```
# Reading the text file 'DRUG-AE.rel' which provides relations
between drugs and adverse effects.
TEXT_FILE = 'DRUG-AE.rel'
```

Next, we want to create input for our model. The input for our model is a sequence of characters. For the time being, we are ascribing a sequence length of 200, i.e., we will have a dataset of size = "number of original characters-sequence length."

For each input data, i.e., 200-character sequence, next, one character will be our output in one-hot encoded format. We will append the input data fields, along with their corresponding labels, in the input_data_ae and op_labels_ae tensors, as follows:

```python
f = open(TEXT_FILE, 'r')

for each_line in f.readlines():
    sent_list = np.zeros([0,200])
    labels = np.zeros([0,3])
    tokens = each_line.split("|")
    sent = tokens[1]
    if sent in sentences:
        continue
    sentences.append(sent)
    begin_offset = int(tokens[3])
    end_offset = int(tokens[4])
    mid_offset = range(begin_offset+1, end_offset)
    word_tokens = nltk.word_tokenize(sent)
    offset = 0
    for each_token in word_tokens:
        offset = sent.find(each_token, offset)
        offset1 = copy.deepcopy(offset)
        offset += len(each_token)
        if each_token in punctuation or re.search(r'\d', each_
        token):
            continue
        each_token = each_token.lower()
        each_token = re.sub("[^A-Za-z\-]+","", each_token)
        if each_token in word2vec.vocab:
            new_word = word2vec.word_vec(each_token)
        if offset1 == begin_offset:
            sent_list = np.append(sent_list, np.array([new_
            word]), axis=0)
            labels = np.append(labels, np.array([[0,0,1]]),
            axis=0)
```

```
        elif offset == end_offset or offset in mid_offset:
            sent_list = np.append(sent_list, np.array([new_
            word]), axis=0)
            labels = np.append(labels, np.array([[0,1,0]]),
            axis=0)
        else:
            sent_list = np.append(sent_list, np.array([new_
            word]), axis=0)
            labels = np.append(labels, np.array([[1,0,0]]),
            axis=0)
    input_data_ae.append(sent_list)
    op_labels_ae.append(labels)
input_data_ae = np.array(input_data_ae)
op_labels_ae  = np.array(op_labels_ae)
```

Add padding to the input text, with the maximum length of the input at any time step being 30 (a safe bet!).

```
input_data_ae = pad_sequences(input_data_ae, maxlen=30,
dtype='float64', padding='post')
op_labels_ae = pad_sequences(op_labels_ae, maxlen=30,
dtype='float64', padding='post')
```

Check the length of the total number of entries in the input data and their corresponding labels.

```
print(len(input_data_ae))
> 4271
print(len(op_labels_ae))
> 4271
```

Import required modules from Keras.

```
from keras.preprocessing.text import Tokenizer
from keras.layers import Dense, Input, LSTM, Embedding,
Dropout, Activation,Bidirectional, TimeDistributed
from keras.layers.merge import concatenate
from keras.models import Model, Sequential
from keras.layers.normalization import BatchNormalization
from keras.callbacks import EarlyStopping, ModelCheckpoint
```

Create train and validation datasets, with 4,000 entries in train, and rest 271 in the validation dataset.

```
# Creating Train and Validation datasets, for 4271 entries,
4000 in train dataset, and 271 in validation dataset
x_train= input_data_ae[:4000]
x_test = input_data_ae[4000:]
y_train = op_labels_ae[:4000]
y_test =op_labels_ae[4000:]
```

As we have the dataset in a standard format now, here comes the most important part of the process: defining the model architecture. We are going to use one hidden layer of a bidirectional LSTM network, with 300 hidden units and a dropout probability of 0.2. In addition to this, we are making use of a TimeDistributedDense layer, with a dropout probability of 0.2.

Dropout is a regularization technique by which, while you're updating layers of your neural net, you randomly don't update, or dropout, some of the layer. That is, while updating your neural net layer, you update each node with a probability of 1-dropout, and leave it unchanged with a probability dropout.

Time distributed layers are used for RNN (and LSTMs) to maintain a one-to-one mapping between input and output. Assume we have 30 time steps with 200 samples of data, i.e., 30 × 200, and we want to use an RNN with an output of 3. If we don't use a TimeDistributedDense layer, we will get a 200 × 30 × 3 tensor. So, we have the output flattened with each time step mixed. If we apply the TimeDistributedDense layer, we are going to apply a fully connected dense layer on each of the time steps and get the output separately by time step.

We are also using `categorical_crossentropy` as a loss function, `adam` as the optimizer, and `softmax` as the activation function.

You can play around with all these things to have a better idea of how an LSTM network works.

```
batch = 1       # Making the batch size as 1, as showing model
                  each of the instances one-by-one
# Adding Bidirectional LSTM with Dropout, and Time Distributed
  layer with Dropout
# Finally using Adam optimizer for training purpose
xin = Input(batch_shape=(batch,30,200), dtype='float')
seq = Bidirectional(LSTM(300, return_sequences=True),merge_
mode='concat')(xin)
mlp1 = Dropout(0.2)(seq)
mlp2 = TimeDistributed(Dense(60, activation='softmax'))(mlp1)
mlp3 = Dropout(0.2)(mlp2)
mlp4 = TimeDistributed(Dense(3, activation='softmax'))(mlp3)
model = Model(inputs=xin, outputs=mlp4)
model.compile(optimizer='Adam', loss='categorical_
crossentropy')
```

We are going to train our model with 50 epochs and a batch size of 1. You can always increase the number of epochs, as long as the model keeps on improving. One can also create checkpoints, so that later, the model can be retrieved and used. The idea behind creating the checkpoint is to save the model weights while training, so that later, you do not have to go through the same process again. This has been left as an exercise for the reader.

```
model.fit(x_train, y_train,
          batch_size=batch,
          epochs=50,
          validation_data=(x_test, y_test))
> Train on 4000 samples, validate on 271 samples
> Epoch 1/50
4000/4000 [==============================] - 363s 91ms/step -
loss: 0.1661 - val_loss: 0.1060
> Epoch 2/50
4000/4000 [==============================] - 363s 91ms/step -
loss: 0.1066 - val_loss: 0.0894
> Epoch 3/50
4000/4000 [==============================] - 361s 90ms/step -
loss: 0.0903 - val_loss: 0.0720
> Epoch 4/50
4000/4000 [==============================] - 364s 91ms/step -
loss: 0.0787 - val_loss: 0.0692
> Epoch 5/50
4000/4000 [==============================] - 362s 91ms/step -
loss: 0.0698 - val_loss: 0.0636
...
...
...
> Epoch 46/50
4000/4000 [==============================] - 344s 86ms/step -
loss: 0.0033 - val_loss: 0.1596
> Epoch 47/50
4000/4000 [==============================] - 321s 80ms/step -
loss: 0.0033 - val_loss: 0.1650
> Epoch 48/50
```

```
4000/4000 [==============================] - 322s 80ms/step -
loss: 0.0036 - val_loss: 0.1684
> Epoch 49/50
4000/4000 [==============================] - 319s 80ms/step -
loss: 0.0027 - val_loss: 0.1751
> Epoch 50/50
4000/4000 [==============================] - 319s 80ms/step -
loss: 0.0035 - val_loss: 0.1666
<keras.callbacks.History at 0x7f48213a3b38>
```

Validating the model results on the validation dataset with 271 entries.

```
val_pred = model.predict(x_test,batch_size=batch)
labels = []
for i in range(len(val_pred)):
    b = np.zeros_like(val_pred[i])
    b[np.arange(len(val_pred[i])), val_pred[i].argmax(1)] = 1
    labels.append(b)

print(val_pred.shape)
> (271, 30, 3)
```

Note   The val_pred tensor is of size (271 × 30 × 3).

Check the model performance using F1-score, along with precision and recall. Import the required modules from the scikit-learn library.

```
from sklearn.metrics import f1_score
from sklearn.metrics import precision_score
from sklearn.metrics import recall_score
```

Define the variables to keep a record of the model performance.

```
score =[]
f1 = []
precision =[]
recall =[]
point = []
```

We can shortlist all the instances in the validation dataset that have an F1-score of more than 0.6. This will give us a fair idea of the performance, with our set benchmark, across the validation data.

```
for i in range(len(y_test)):
    if(f1_score(labels[i],y_test[i],average='weighted')>.6):
        point.append(i)
    score.append(f1_score(labels[i],
    y_test[i],average='weighted'))
    precision.append(precision_score(labels[i],
    y_test[i],average='weighted'))
    recall.append(recall_score(labels[i],
    y_test[i],average='weighted'))
print(len(point)/len(labels)*100)
> 69.37
print(np.mean(score))
> 0.686
print(np.mean(precision))
> 0.975
print(np.mean(recall))
> 0.576
```

Although the result produced is not quite satisfying, it does achieve near state-of-the-art results. These limitations could be overcome by building a denser network, increasing the number of epochs and the length of the dataset.

Training large datasets using CPU takes too much time. That's why using GPU has been almost inevitable and very important for quickly training deep learning models.

Training an RNN is a fun exercise. The same algorithm can be extended for many other exercises, such as music generation, speech generation, etc. It can also be efficiently extended to real-life applications, such as video captioning and language translation.

We encourage the reader to create their own models for diverse applications at this level. We will be covering a lot more of such examples in the next chapters.

Next Steps

The structures presented in this chapter are its most important part and the core of any RNN type, be it Siamese networks, seq2seq models, attention mechanisms, or transfer learning. (Readers are advised to take a further look into these concepts, for a better understanding of the widely available networks, the variations in their structures, and their respective use cases.)

Further, if you can intuit how the dimension and multiplication of 3-D vectors work in TensorFlow and NumPy, you are very capable of implementing the most complex models. So, the focus should be on grasping the basics as much as you can. Models aiming to increase the complexity with attention/weights are just a few more iterations/thinking to improve the model accuracy. These further improvements are more like hacks, however successful, but still require a structured thought process. The best recourse, again, is to keep on trying different types of models and their wide applications, to gain a good hold on the concepts.

CHAPTER 4

Developing a Chatbot

In this chapter, we will create a chatbot. We will do so in a progressive manner and will make the chatbot in two layers. The first section of the chapter introduces the chatbot concept, followed by a section on implementing a basic rule-based chatbot system. The last section discusses the training of a sequence-to-sequence (seq2seq) recurrent neural network (RNN) model on a publicly available dataset. The final chatbot will be able to answer specific questions asked of the dataset domain on which the model has been trained. We hope that you have enjoyed the previous chapters, and this chapter, as well, will keep you involved in the implementation of deep learning and natural language processing (NLP).

Introduction to Chatbot

The fact that we all are using a chatbot, even without knowing exactly how to define it, makes the idea of a chatbot's definition irrelevant.

We all are using a variety of apps in our day-to-day life, and it would be astonishing if someone reading this chapter had not heard about "chatbots." Chatbots are just like any other app. The only thing that separates chatbots from regular apps is their user interface. Chatbots have

© Palash Goyal, Sumit Pandey, Karan Jain 2018
P. Goyal, et al., *Deep Learning for Natural Language Processing*,
https://doi.org/10.1007/978-1-4842-3685-7_4

a chat interface, whereby the user literally chats, rather, messages, with the app and operates it in a conversational manner, instead of a visual interface, composed of buttons and icons. We hope the definition is clear for now and that you can deep-dive into the wonderful world of chatbots.

Origin of Chatbots

Just like the fact that we hate the idea of origin, we love the idea of origin.

> *Don't become a mere recorder of facts, but try to penetrate the mystery of their origin.*
>
> —Ivan Pavlov

It would not be useful to cover chatbots without exploring their origin. You may be amused by the fact that in 1950, when the world was recovering from the shock of World War II, Alan Turing, an English polymath, had the foresight to develop a test to see if a person could distinguish a human from a machine. This is know as the Turing test (`https://en.wikipedia.org/wiki/Turing_test`).

Sixteen years later, in 1966, a computer program called ELIZA was invented by Joseph Weizenbaum. It imitated the language of a psychotherapist from only 200 lines of code. You can still talk with it here: `http://psych.fullerton.edu/mbirnbaum/psych101/Eliza.htm`.

```
Talk to Eliza
> Hello, I am Eliza.
* hi how are you?
> Why are you interested in whether or not I am ?




Input:
```

Recent developments in machine learning have powered chatbots as never before, interpreting natural language to both understand and learn better over time. Major corporations, such as Facebook, Apple, Google (Alphabet), and Microsoft, are devoting significant resources to research related to imitating real-life conversations between consumers and machines, with commercially viable business models.

But How Does a Chatbot Work, Anyway?

OK, enough introduction. Let's get to the point.

> *"Hey, what's up?"*

> *"How're you doing?"*

> *"Hello!"*

These sentences seem familiar. Don't they? They are all messages, of one kind or another, to greet someone. How do we respond to these greetings? Typically, we respond with "I am good. How about you?"

This is exactly how chatbots work. A typical chatbot finds the so-called context of the question asked, which, in this case, is the "greeting." The bot then picks up the appropriate response and sends it back to the user. How does it find the appropriate response, and can it deal with such attachments as image, audio, and video? We will deal with that in the following sections.

Why Are Chatbots Such a Big Opportunity?

Research conducted by Forrester (`https://go.forrester.com/data/consumer-technographics/`) points out that about ~85 percent of our time on mobile devices is spent on the major applications, such as e-mail and messaging platforms. With the great benefits offered by deep learning and NLP, almost every firm is trying to build applications to keep their potential consumers engaged with their products and services, and chatbots uniquely serve that purpose.Multiple human errors and customer requests handled by a conventional customer care service could be easily avoided by putting chatbots in place. Moreover, chatbots could allow a customer and a concerned company to have access to all the previous chat/issue records.

Although a chatbot could be considered an application that conducts a conversation with an end customer, the tasks and few concerned applications performed by a chatbot could be classified at a higher level, under the following categories:

- *Question answering*: One turn per user; useful when a labeled answer is present

    a) Product querying use cases

    b) Extracting user information

- *Sentence completion*: Filling in of the missing word in the next utterance in a dialog

  a) Mapping of right product to the customer

- *Goal-oriented dialog*: Conversation with the task of achieving a goal

  a) Recommendation to the customer

  b) Negotiating a price with the customer

- *Chit-chat dialog*: Conversations having no explicit goals, more of a discussion

  No such use case to focus now

- *Visual dialog*: Tasks with texts, images, and audio

  a) Exchanging images with customers and building inferences on those

OK, you may now be thinking, "I am excited. How can I build one?"

Building a Chatbot Can Sound Intimidating. Is It Actually?

The difficulty in building a Chatbot is less a technical one and more of user experience. One of the most prevalent successful bots in market are the ones that users want to come back to regularly and that provide consistent value to their daily tasks and requirements.

—Matt Hartman, Director of Seed Investments at Betaworks

Prior to building a chatbot, it makes more sense if we resolve the following four questions in advance and then decide how we want to take the project forward:

- What problem are we going to solve with the bot?

- Which platform will our bot will live on (Facebook, Slack, etc.)?

- What server we will be using to host the bot? Heroku (`www.heroku.com`) or our own?

- Do we want to start from scratch or use the available chatbot platform tools (following)?

  - Botsify (`https://botsify.com/`)

  - Pandorabots (`https://playground.pandorabots.com/en/`)

  - Chattypeople (`www.chattypeople.com/`)

  - Wit.ai (`https://wit.ai/`)

  - Api.ai (`https://api.ai/`)

To gain a deeper understanding of the working methodology of the different platforms and the best fit as per the use case of the business, one can refer to the following documentations from the following links to some popular chatbot platforms:

- Facebook Messenger (`https://developers.facebook.com/products/messenger/`)

- Slack (`https://api.slack.com/bot-users`)

- Discord (`https://blog.discordapp.com/the-robot-revolution-has-unofficially-begun/`)

- Telegram (`https://core.telegram.org/bots/api`)

- Kik (`https://dev.kik.com/#/home`)

Conversational Bot

For the first version of our conversational chatbot, we will be making a rule-based bot that will help the developer to define his/her desired answers to a specific category of questions asked by the end user. Creating such a bot will help us to have a basic understanding of working with bots, before we proceed to the next level, with text-generating bots.

We will be using Facebook Messenger as our desired platform and Heroku as our desired server, to launch the basic version of chatbot. First things first. You must have a Facebook page. If you don't have one, please create one. To communicate with a bot, one must access this page and select the messaging option, to initiate the conversation.

Follow the steps in Figure 4-1 to create the page on Facebook:

1. Select the Create a Page option.

2. Select the desired category of the organization and choose a name to create the page. We have selected Insurance as the field of the organization, as later on, we will build test cases around it and use an Insurance-related conversation dataset to train our model.

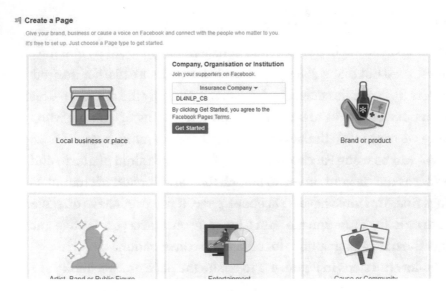

Figure 4-1. *Creating a Facebook page*

3. Add a profile and cover photo, as desired, for the page.

After performing the preceding steps, the final page, Dl4nlp_cb, `www.facebook.com/dlnlpcb/`, will look like Figure 4-2.

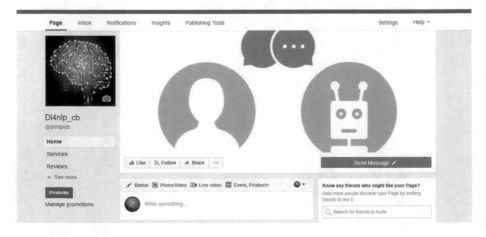

Figure 4-2. *Dl4nlp_cb Facebook page*

The next step is to create a Facebook app. Visit the following URL to create one, with your official Facebook account logged in: `https://developers.facebook.com/apps/`. This app will subscribe to the created page and will handle all the responses on behalf of that page (Figure 4-3).

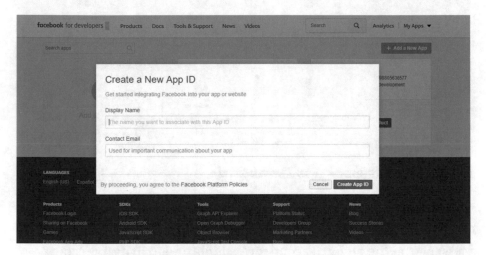

Figure 4-3. *Creating a Facebook app*

We have assigned the same display name to the app as to the previously created Facebook page and have registered it with the desired e-mail ID. Post the app creation. The App Dashboard will look like that in Figure 4-4.

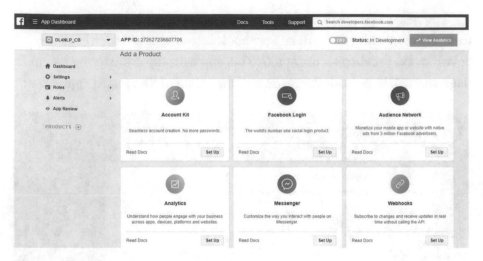

Figure 4-4. *Facebook App Dashboard*

Facebook offers a range of products that can be added to the newly created app. For the purpose of the chatbot, we are required to select Messenger as the option (second row, middle option in the preceding image). Click the Set Up button. This will redirect the user to the Settings page (Figure 4-5), from which, in addition to selecting tutorials, we can create the token and set up webhooks (covered following).

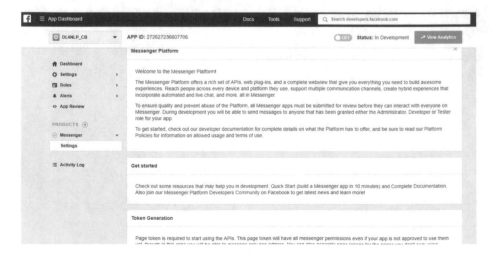

Figure 4-5. *Facebook app Settings page*

From the Settings page, go to the Token Generation section and select the page created in the first step. An alert box will pop up and ask to grant permissions. Click Continue and proceed (Figure 4-6).

Figure 4-6. *Facebook Token Generation*

Note   One can check the information being accessed by Facebook regarding this application. Click the Review the info that you provide link to check it.

After selecting the Continue option, you will get another window that displays the permissions being granted to the page. Users can select the privileges to be granted. For the current purpose, it is recommended not to change any of the previously selected options in the privilege section (Figure 4-7).

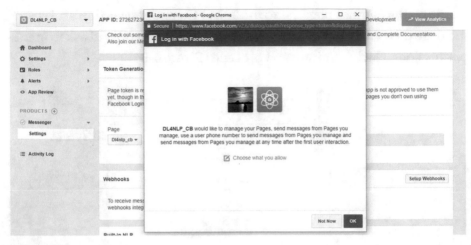

Figure 4-7. *Privilege grant section*

Clicking Choose what you allow will show the permissions granted to the page. After checking it, click OK and move to additional steps (Figure 4-8).

Figure 4-8. *Permissions granted*

This will initiate the generation of the token on the app Settings page (it might take a few seconds to generate the token). See Figure 4-9.

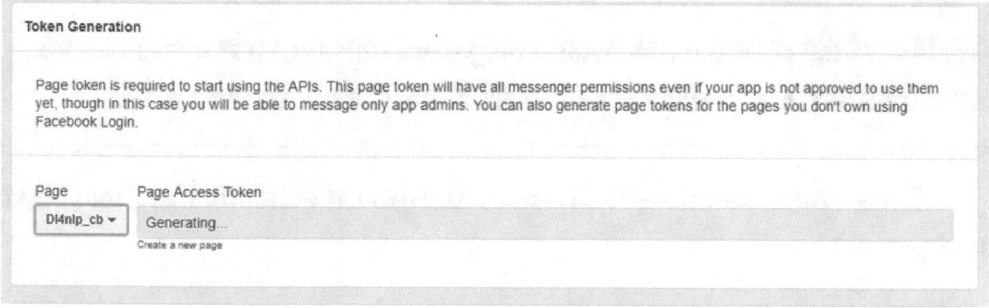

Token Generation

Page token is required to start using the APIs. This page token will have all messenger permissions even if your app is not approved to use them yet, though in this case you will be able to message only app admins. You can also generate page tokens for the pages you don't own using Facebook Login.

Page | Page Access Token
DI4nlp_cb ▼ | Generating...
Create a new page

Figure 4-9. *Final page access token generation*

The page access token is a long string, combination of numbers, and alphabets that we will use later to create the application with Heroku. It will be set as a configuration parameter in the Heroku application.

The token is unique to every time it is generated and will be separate for each application, page, and user combination. After generation, it will look like the one in Figure 4-10.

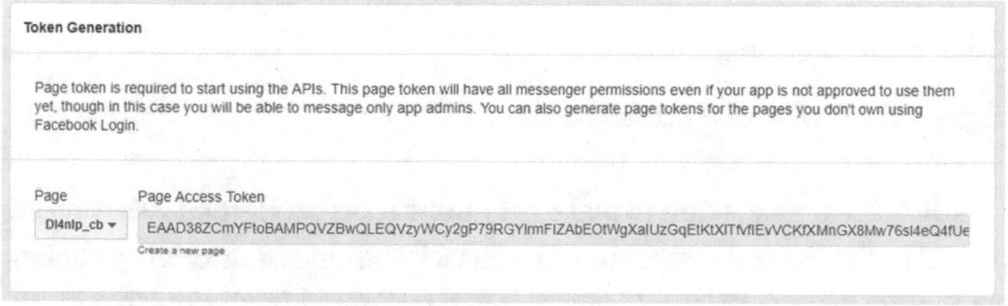

Token Generation

Page token is required to start using the APIs. This page token will have all messenger permissions even if your app is not approved to use them yet, though in this case you will be able to message only app admins. You can also generate page tokens for the pages you don't own using Facebook Login.

Page | Page Access Token
DI4nlp_cb ▼ | EAAD38ZCmYFtoBAMPQVZBwQLEQVzyWCy2gP79RGYlrmFIZAbEOtWgXaIUzGqEtKtXITfvflEvVCKfXMnGX8Mw76sI4eQ4fUe
Create a new page

Figure 4-10. *Page access token*

After creating the Facebook page and app, register and open an account on Heroku (`www.heroku.com`) and create an app here as well, with Python as the chosen language.

Creating an app on Heroku will provide us a webhook, to which the Facebook app will send the request, in case an event is triggered, i.e., for chatbot, whenever some message is received or sent.

Note   Make sure the password being used for Heroku is a combination of letters, numbers, and symbols—all three, not merely two.

After account creation, the Heroku dashboard will look like that shown in Figure 4-11.

Figure 4-11. *Heroku dashboard*

Click Create New App to make the application on Heroku. For tutorials related to the Python language, one can visit the shared tutorial by clicking the Python button: `https://devcenter.heroku.com/articles/getting-started-with-python#introduction`. For now, keep the default selection of "United States," as it is, and for pipeline, don't make any selection while creating the app (Figure 4-12).

Note   The name of the app cannot contain numbers, underscores, or symbols. Only lowercase letters are allowed in the app name.

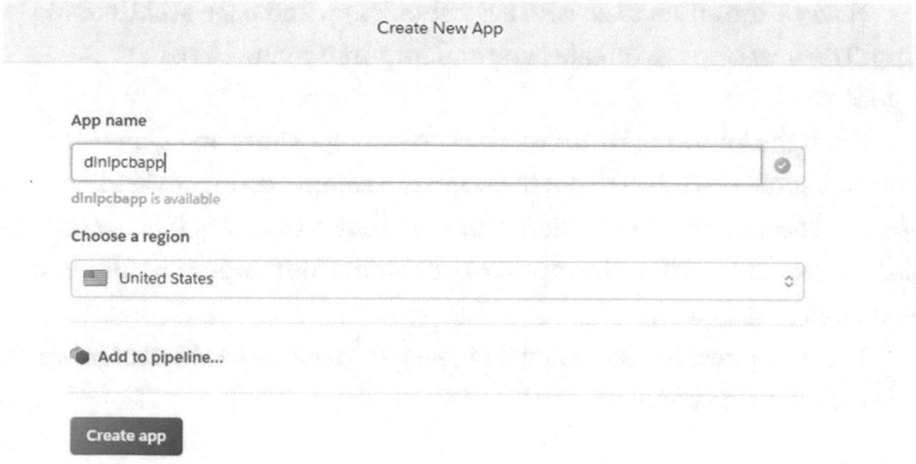

Figure 4-12. *Heroku app creation*

The Heroku application dashboard will look like that in Figure 4-13, and by default, the Deploy tab is selected after app creation.

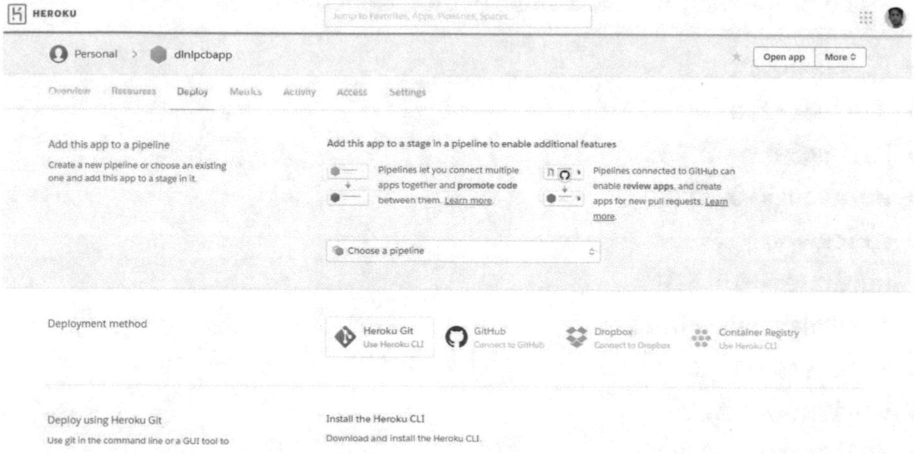

Figure 4-13. *Heroku app dashboard*

Now we are all set to go with a Facebook app and page and Heroku app. The next step is to create code and import it in the Heroku application.

From the following URL, visit the GitHub repository and clone it to your personal GitHub account to access the sample code provided for the test cases on the first version of our chatbot: `https://github.com/palashgoyal1/DL4NLP`. The repository contains four important files that you need to start with.

The **.gitignore file** tells Git which files (or patterns) it should ignore. It has the following content:

```
> *.pyc
> .*
```

Procfile is used to declare various process types, in our case, a web app.

```
> web: gunicorn app:app --log-file=-
```

The **Requirements.txt** installs Python dependencies.

```
> Flask==0.11.1
> Jinja2==2.8
> MarkupSafe==0.23
> Werkzeug==0.11.10
> click==6.6
> gunicorn==19.6.0
> itsdangerous==0.24
> requests==2.10.0
> wsgiref==0.1.2
> chatterbot>=0.4.6
> urllib
> clarifai==2.0.30
> enum34
```

App.py is the Python file containing the main code for the chatbot application. As the file is big, we have put it on the GitHub repository previously mentioned. Readers are requested to visit it for reference. That way, it will be easier to clone the repository as well.

Let's set the webhook. (A webhook is an HTTP callback—an HTTP POST that occurs when something happens, such as a simple event-notification via HTTP POST.) We have used Heroku because it provides a webhook that Facebook uses to send a request and retrieve the appropriate result, in case of any event.

Visit the app you created in Heroku and then go to the Deploy tab. There are four methods via which you can deploy your app via Heroku Git, via GitHub, via Dropbox, and via Container Registry (Figure 4-14). To keep things simple, we will deploy our code using GitHub.

Figure 4-14. *Heroku deploy app section*

Once we select Connect to GitHub, it will ask for the GitHub repository where the code has been placed. Make sure the name mentioned here is correct and the home directory as the repository. Click the Connect button, after selecting the correct repository (Figure 4-15).

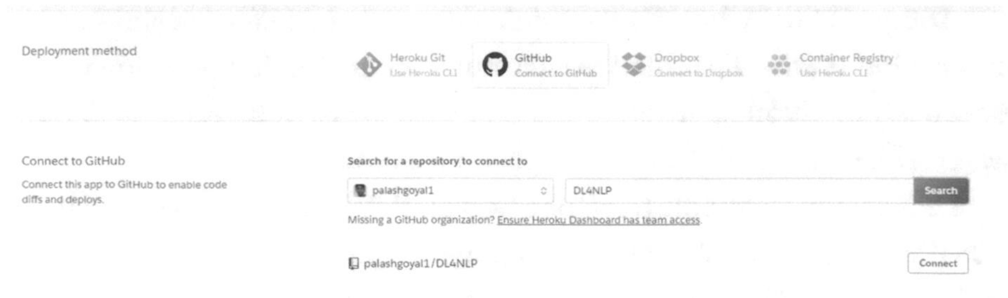

Figure 4-15. *Heroku deploy app via GitHub*

The code will be deployed using the link of your personal GitHub repository for this particular app, where the code has been placed. From the Settings tab in Heroku, you can find the domain name of the app, under the Domains and Certificates subsection, which looks similar in format to `https://*******.herokuapp.com/`. For the test application created previously, it is `https://dlnlpcbapp.herokuapp.com/`. Note it down separately, as we will need it later.

Now is the time to integrate the Facebook page Dl4nlp_cb and the Heroku app dlnlpcbapp. Visit the Facebook App Dashboard and, under the Messenger Settings tab where the page access token is displayed, go to webhooks to set up the webhook (Figure 4-16).

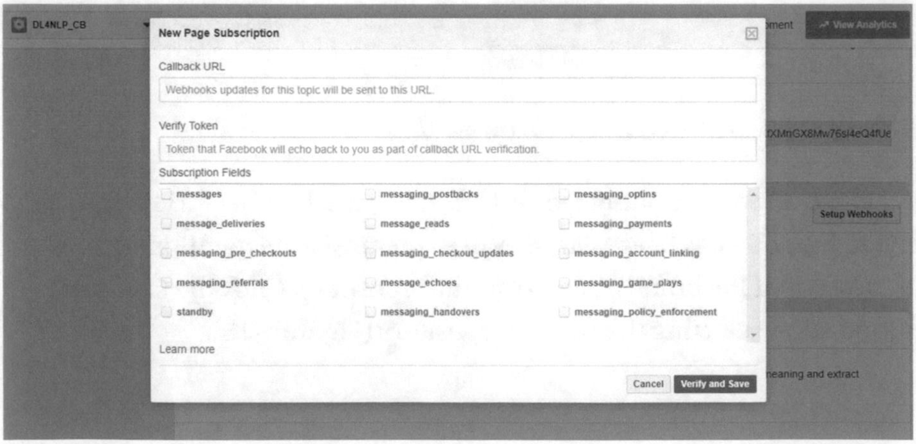

Figure 4-16. *Setting the webhook*

The pop-up will ask for the following three fields:

- **Callback URL**: The Heroku URL that we set up earlier (the setup URL that we generated in step 1)

- **Verification Token**: A secret value that will be sent to your bot, in order to verify that the request is coming from Facebook. Whatever value you set here, make sure you add it to your Heroku environment.

- **Subscription Fields**: This tells Facebook what messaging events you care about and want it to notify your webhook about. If you're not sure, check all the boxes (Figure 4-17).

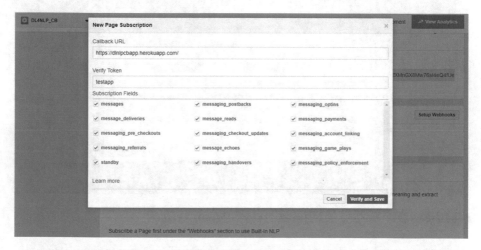

Figure 4-17. *Setting the webhook—adding relevant information*

Note   "Callback verification failed" is one of the most common errors reported, and it is encountered when Facebook returns an error message (Figure 4-18) when trying to add the Heroku endpoint to the Facebook chat application.

Flask application intentionally returns a 403 Forbidden error if the token that Facebook sends doesn't match the token set using the Heroku configuration variables.

If the error shown in Figure 4-18 is encountered, it means that the Heroku config values were not set properly. Running `heroku config` from the command line within the application and verifying that the key called `VERIFY_TOKEN` is set equal to the value typed in the Facebook window will rectify the error.

The URL shown in the Callback URL box, will be the Heroku application URL.

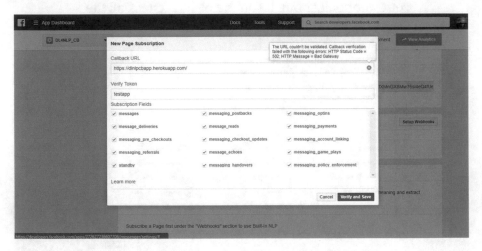

Figure 4-18. *Error: "Callback verification failed"*

A successful configuration of the webhook will take you to another screen showing the completion message (Figure 4-19).

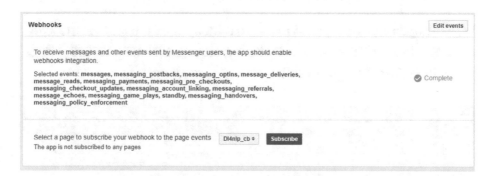

Figure 4-19. *Successful webhook configuration*

After you've configured your webhook, select the desired Facebook page and click Subscribe (Figure 4-20).

Figure 4-20. *Subscribe webhook to desired Facebook page Dl4nlp_cb*

Now go back again to the Heroku app. Under the Settings tab, you will find "config variable option." You will have to set two variables: PAGE_ACCESS_TOKEN (pick it from earlier steps) and VERIFY_TOKEN (pick it from the one used while setting up the webhook in App Dashboard). In addition to the preceding two parameters, fetch as well the App ID and Api Secret token from the Basic Settings of the App page (Figure 4-21). These two must also be set in the Heroku configuration parameters (click the Show button to get the Api Secret token).

Figure 4-21. *Configuring Heroku settings*

Now open the Settings tab in the Heroku application and set the App ID as `api_key`, APP Secret as `api_secret`, along with `PAGE_ACCESS_TOKEN` and `VERIFY_TOKEN` (Figure 4-22).

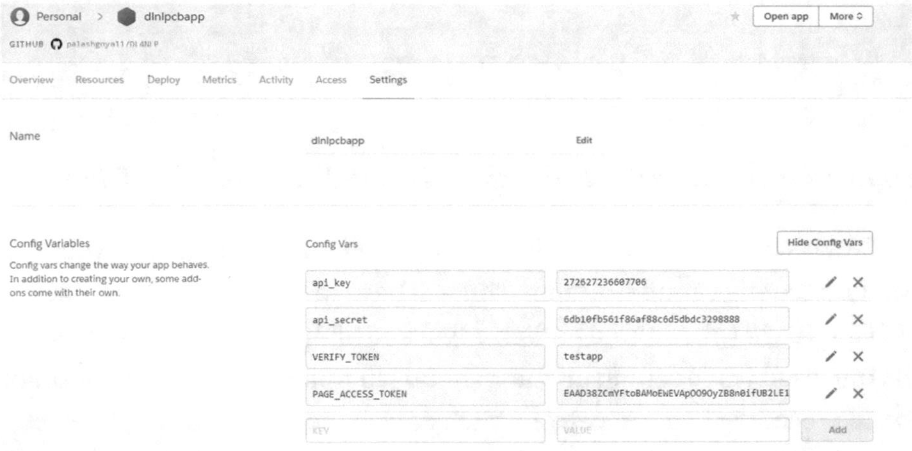

Figure 4-22. *Adding configuration variables in Heroku settings*

After saving the configuration parameters, go to the Deploy tab on Heroku, scroll down to the Manual Deploy section, and click the Deploy Branch button. This will deploy the current branch being selected from the repository and do the necessary compilations. Make sure that there are no errors, by checking the Logs section.

Now go to the created Facebook page and click the Message button, next to the Like button, near the top of the page. This should open a message pane with the message box of your page. Start chatting with your custom-made chatbot (Figure 4-23)!

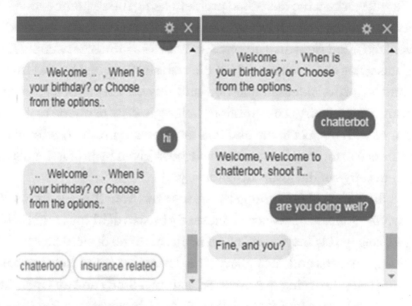

Figure 4-23. *Enjoy your conversations with the chatbot!*

Chatbot: Automatic Text Generation

In the previous section, we built a simple conversational chatbot using different platforms and libraries. The problem with it is that it can handle only a fixed set of questions. What if we can build a bot that learns from existing conversations, between humans. This is where *natural language generation* comes in handy. We will make a seq2seq model that can handle

191

any type of questions, i.e., even if the question is composed of some random set of words. Whether that answer will be grammatically and contextually correct is a whole different issue and will depend on various factors, such as the size and quality of the dataset.

In this section, we will attempt to build a model that takes a set of questions and answers as input and predicts the answer when asked a question related to the input data. The question will be answered in the best possible manner if it matches the set of questions being used to train the model.

We will work on the described problem using the sequence-to-sequence models. The dataset we are using is composed of questions-and-answers recorded from an insurance domain's customer service station. The dataset has been collected from the web site `www.insurancelibrary.com/` and is the first released question-and-answer corpus of its type in the insurance industry. The questions belong to a set of queries asked by customers with respect to the multiple services and products offered by an insurance firm, and the answers have been given by professionals with deep knowledge of the insurance industry.

The dataset used for training has been taken from the URL `https://github.com/shuzi/insuranceQA`, presently hosted at `https://github.com/palashgoyal1/InsuranceQnA`, in addition to the desired files for questions, answers, and vocabulary. The dataset was used in the paper "Applying Deep Learning to Answer Selection: A Study and an Open Task" (`https://arxiv.org/pdf/1508.01585v2.pdf`), by several staff at IBM, and they have used the CNN framework with multiple variations. In all the variations, they have made the model learn the word embedding of a given question and its corresponding answer, and then used cosine distance as a similarity metric to measure the matching degree.

Figure 4-24 is a snapshot of the multiple architectures being demonstrated in the paper. For Architectures II, III, and IV, the questions-and-answers sides share the same weights for the hidden and CNN layers.

The CNN_Q and CNN_A layers are used to extract the questions-and-answers sides' features, respectively.

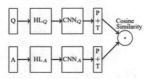

Architecture I . Q for question; A for answer; P is 1-MaxPooling; T is *tanh* layer; HL for hidden layer and HL already includes *tanh* as its activation function.

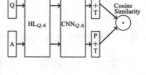

Architecture II . QA means the weights of corresponding layer are shared by Q and A .

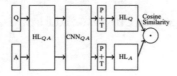

Architecture III . HL for hidden layer. Add another HL_Q and HL_A after CNN_{QA} .

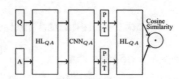

Architecture IV . Add another shared hidden layer HL_{QA} after CNN_{QA} .

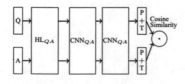

Architecture V . Two shared CNN_{QA} .

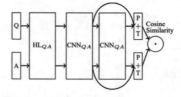

Architecture VI . Two shared CNN_{QA} . Two cost functions.

Figure 4-24. *Architectures used in the research paper*

The original dataset present in the GitHub repository has a combination of the train, validation, and test partitions of the questions. We have combined the given questions and answers and have performed a few processing steps before making the final selection of the QnAs to be selected for the modeling purpose. Also, a set of sequence-to-sequence models has been used to generate the answers to the questions being asked by the user. If trained using the appropriate model, and with enough iterations, the model will be able to answer previously unseen questions as well.

To prepare the data to be used by the model, we have made a few changes and completed the selection on the initial given dataset. Later, we made use of the overall dataset vocabulary, and the word tokens used in questions and answers, to create the perfect combination of questions and their corresponding answers in an understandable format in the English language.

Note   Before starting the code execution, make sure that you have TensorFlow version 1.0.0 installed and no other version, as there have been changes in the later updated versions of TensorFlow.

Import the required packages and dataset in the encoded formats.

```
import pandas as pd
import numpy as np
import tensorflow as tf
import re
import time
tf.__version__
```

```
> '1.0.0'
```

```
# Make sure the vocabulary.txt file and the encoded datasets
for Question and Answer are present in the same folder
# reading vocabulary
lines = open('vocabulary.txt', encoding='utf-8',
errors='ignore').read().split('\n')
# reading questions
conv_lines = open('InsuranceQAquestionanslabelraw.encoded',
encoding='utf-8', errors='ignore').read().split('\n')
# reading answers
conv_lines1 = open('InsuranceQAlabel2answerraw.encoded',
encoding='utf-8', errors='ignore').read().split('\n')

# The print command shows the token value associated with each
of the words in the 3 datasets
```

```
print(" -- Vocabulary -- ")
print(lines[:2])
```

```
> -- Vocabulary -
> ['idx_17904\trating/result', 'idx_14300\tconsidered,']
```

```
print(" -- Questions -- ")
print(conv_lines[:2])
```

```
> -- Questions -
> ['medicare-insurance\tidx_1285 idx_1010 idx_467 idx_47610
idx_18488 idx_65760\t16696', 'long-term-care-insurance\
tidx_3815 idx_604 idx_605 idx_891 idx_136 idx_5293 idx_65761\
t10277']
```

```
print(" -- Answers -- ")
print(conv_lines1[:2])
```

```
> -- Answers -
> ['1\tidx_1 idx_2 idx_3 idx_4 idx_5 idx_6 idx_7 idx_8 idx_9
idx_10 idx_11 idx_12 idx_13 idx_14 idx_3 idx_12 idx_15 idx_16
idx_17 idx_8 idx_18 idx_19 idx_20 idx_21 idx_3 idx_12 idx_14
idx_22 idx_20 idx_23 idx_24 idx_25 idx_26 idx_27 idx_28 idx_29
idx_8 idx_30 idx_19 idx_11 idx_4 idx_31 idx_32 idx_22 idx_33
idx_34 idx_35 idx_36 idx_37 idx_30 idx_38 idx_39 idx_11 idx_40
idx_41 idx_42 idx_43 idx_44 idx_22 idx_45 idx_46 ...
```

In the next few lines, we have combined the questions with their corresponding answers on the basis of the ID being allocated to both questions and answers.

```
id2line = {}
for line in vocab_lines:
    _line = line.split('\t')
    if len(_line) == 2:
        id2line[_line[0]] = _line[1]
```

```
# Creating the word tokens for both questions and answers,
along with the mapping of the answers enlisted for questions
convs, ansid = [], []
for line in question_lines[:-1]:
    _line = line.split('\t')
    ansid.append(_line[2].split(' '))
    convs.append(_line[1])

convs1 = [ ]
for line in answer_lines[:-1]:
    _line = line.split('\t')
    convs1.append(_line[1])

print(convs[:2])  # word tokens present in the question
> ['idx_1285 idx_1010 idx_467 idx_47610 idx_18488 idx_65760',
'idx_3815 idx_604 idx_605 idx_891 idx_136 idx_5293 idx_65761']

print(ansid[:2])  # answers IDs mapped to the questions
> [['16696'], ['10277']]

print(convs1[:2])  # word tokens present in the answer
> ['idx_1 idx_2 idx_3 idx_4 idx_5 idx_6 idx_7 idx_8 idx_9
idx_10 idx_11 idx_12 idx_13 idx_14 idx_3 idx_12 idx_15 idx_16
idx_17 idx_8 idx_18 idx_19 idx_20 idx_21 ...

# Creating matching pair between questions and answers on the
basis of the ID allocated to each.
questions, answers = [], []
for a in range(len(ansid)):
    for b in range(len(ansid[a])):
        questions.append(convs[a])

for a in range(len(ansid)):
    for b in range(len(ansid[a])):
        answers.append(convs1[int(ansid[a][b])-1])
```

```
ques, ans  =[], []
m=0
while m<len(questions):
       i=0
       a=[]
       while i < (len(questions[m].split(' '))):
             a.append(id2line[questions[m].split(' ')[i]])
             i=i+1
       ques.append(' '.join(a))
       m=m+1

n=0
while n<len(answers):
       j=0
       b=[]
       while j < (len(answers[n].split(' '))):
             b.append(id2line[answers[n].split(' ')[j]])
             j=j+1
       ans.append(' '.join(b))
       n=n+1
```

The following output of the top-five questions in the Insurance QnA dataset will give an idea of the kind of questions being asked by the customers and the respective answers given by the professionals. At the end of this exercise, our model will try to provide answers in a similar manner as the questions asked.

```
# Printing top 5 questions along with their answers
limit = 0
for i in range(limit, limit+5):
    print(ques[i])
    print(ans[i])
    print("---")
```

> What Does Medicare IME Stand For?

According to the Centers for Medicare and Medicaid Services website, cms.gov, IME stands for Indirect Medical Education and is in regards to payment calculation adjustments for a Medicare discharge of higher cost patients receiving care from teaching hospitals relative to non-teaching hospitals. I would recommend contacting CMS to get more information about IME

> Is Long Term Care Insurance Tax Free?

As a rule, if you buy a tax qualified long term care insurance policy (as nearly all are, these days), and if you are paying the premium yourself, there are tax advantages you will receive. If you are self employed, the entire premium is tax deductible. If working somewhere but paying your own premium for an individual or group policy, you can deduct the premium as a medical expense under the same IRS rules as apply to all medical expenses. In both situations, you also receive the benefits from the policy tax free, if they are ever needed.

> Can Husband Drop Wife From Health Insurance?

Can a spouse drop another spouse from health insurance? Usually not without the spouse's who is being dropped consent in writting. Most employers who have a quality HR department will require a paper trial for any changes in an employee's benefit plan. When changes are attempted that could come back to haunt the employer, steps are usually taken to comfirm something like this.

> Is Medicare Run By The Government?

Medicare Part A and Part B is provided by the Federal government for Americans who are 65 and older who have worked and paid Social Security taxes into the system. Medicare is

also available to people under the age of 65 that have certain disabilities and people with End-Stage Renal Disease (ESRD).

> Is Medicare Run By The Government?
Definitely. It is ran by the Center for Medicare and Medicaid Services, a Government Agency given the responsibility of overseeing and administering Medicare and Medicaid. Even Medicare Advantage Plans, which are administered by private insurance companies are strongly regulated by CMMS. They work along with Social Security and Jobs and Family Services to insure that your benefits are available and properly administered.

Although the fourth and fifth questions in the preceding sample are the same, they have different answers, depending on how many professionals have answered the question.

```
# Checking the count of the total number of questions and
answers
print(len(questions))
>  27987

print(len(answers))
>  27987
```

Create a text cleaning function by replacing the short forms of the words with the actual extended words, so that the words can be replaced later by their actual tokens.

```
def clean_text(text):
        """Cleaning the text by replacing the abbreviated words
with their proper full replacement, and converting all the
characters to lower case"""

        text = text.lower()
```

```python
        text = re.sub(r"i'm", "i am", text)
        text = re.sub(r"he's", "he is", text)
        text = re.sub(r"she's", "she is", text)
        text = re.sub(r"it's", "it is", text)
        text = re.sub(r"that's", "that is", text)
        text = re.sub(r"what's", "that is", text)
        text = re.sub(r"where's", "where is", text)
        text = re.sub(r"how's", "how is", text)
        text = re.sub(r"\'ll", " will", text)
        text = re.sub(r"\'ve", " have", text)
        text = re.sub(r"\'re", " are", text)
        text = re.sub(r"\'d", " would", text)
        text = re.sub(r"\'re", " are", text)
        text = re.sub(r"won't", "will not", text)
        text = re.sub(r"can't", "cannot", text)
        text = re.sub(r"n't", " not", text)
        text = re.sub(r"n'", "ng", text)
        text = re.sub(r"'bout", "about", text)
        text = re.sub(r"'til", "until", text)
        text = re.sub(r"[-()\"#/@;:<>{}`+=~|.!?,']", "", text)

        return text


# Applying the 'clean_text()' function on the set of Questions
and Answers
clean_questions = []
for question in ques:
    clean_questions.append(clean_text(question))

clean_answers = []
for answer in ans:
    clean_answers.append(clean_text(answer))
```

Take a look at how the dataset appears after performing the cleaning operation on both questions and answers. This cleaned dataset will be fed as input to our model, to ensure that the inputs given to the model are synchronous with each other in their structure and format:

```
limit = 0
for i in range(limit, limit+5):
    print(clean_questions[i])
    print(clean_answers[i])
    print()
```

```
> what does medicare ime stand for
according to the centers for medicare and medicaid services
website cmsgov ime stands for indirect medical education and is
in regards to payment calculation adjustments for a medicare
discharge of higher cost patients receiving care from teaching
hospitals relative to nonteaching hospitals i would recommend
contacting cms to get more information about ime
----
> is long term care insurance tax free
as a rule if you buy a tax qualified long term care insurance
policy as nearly all are these days and if you are paying the
premium yourself there are tax advantages you will receive if
you are self employed the entire premium is tax deductible if
working somewhere but paying your own premium for an individual
or group policy you can deduct the premium as a medical expense
under the same irs rules as apply to all medical expenses in
both situations you also receive the benefits from the policy
tax free if they are ever needed
----
> can husband drop wife from health insurance
can a spouse drop another spouse from health insurance usually
not without the spouses who is being dropped consent in
```

writting most employers who have a quality hr department will require a paper trial for any changes in an employees benefit plan when changes are attempted that could come back to haunt the employer steps are usually taken to comfirm something like this

----

> is medicare run by the government
medicare part a and part b is provided by the federal government for americans who are 65 and older who have worked and paid social security taxes into the system medicare is also available to people under the age of 65 that have certain disabilities and people with endstage renal disease esrd

----

> is medicare run by the government
definitely it is ran by the center for medicare and medicaid services a government agency given the responsibility of overseeing and administering medicare and medicaid even medicare advantage plans which are administered by private insurance companies are strongly regulated by cmms they work along with social security and jobs and family services to insure that your benefits are available and properly administered

----

Analyze the questions and answers on the basis of the number of words coming in for both and checking the percentiles for different intervals.

```
lengths.describe(percentiles=[0,0.25,0.5,0.75,0.85,0.9,0.95,0.99])
```

```
>              counts
      count  55974.000000
      mean    54.176725
```

std	67.638972
min	2.000000
0%	2.000000
25%	7.000000
50%	30.000000
75%	78.000000
85%	103.000000
90%	126.000000
95%	173.000000
99%	314.000000
max	1176.000000

As the data being fed to the model requires the full answer to the asked question, and not a half-baked one, we must make sure that the questions-and-answers combination we are selecting for the model training have a sufficient number of words presented across both questions and answers, thereby putting a minimum cap on the word count. At the same time, we want the model to produce concise and to-the-point answers to the questions, so we are putting the maximum cap on the count of words in questions and answers as well.

Here, we are shortlisting only the text with a minimum of two words and a maximum of 100 words.

```
# Remove questions and answers that are shorter than 1 words
and longer than 100 words.
min_line_length, max_line_length = 2, 100

# Filter out the questions that are too short/long
short_questions_temp, short_answers_temp = [], []
```

```
i = 0
for question in clean_questions:
    if len(question.split()) >= min_line_length and
    len(question.split()) <= max_line_length:
        short_questions_temp.append(question)
        short_answers_temp.append(clean_answers[i])
    i += 1

# Filter out the answers that are too short/long
short_questions, short_answers = [], []

i = 0
for answer in short_answers_temp:
    if len(answer.split()) >= min_line_length and len(answer.
    split()) <= max_line_length:
        short_answers.append(answer)
        short_questions.append(short_questions_temp[i])
    i += 1
```

Dataset stats after performing the preceding selection follow:

```
print("# of questions:", len(short_questions))
> # of questions: 19108
```

```
print("# of answers:", len(short_answers))
> # of answers: 19108
```

```
print("% of data used: {}%".format(round(len(short_questions)/
len(questions),4)*100))
> % of data used: 68.27%
```

The problem with directly feeding the text input is that the model cannot handle *variable length sequences*, and the next big problem is the *vocabulary size*. The decoder has to run softmax over a large vocabulary, say, 20,000 words, for each word in the output. This will slow down the training process. So, how do we deal with this problem? **Padding**.

Padding is a way to convert a variable length sequence into a fixed length sequence. Assuming we want the sentence "How are you?" to be of a fixed length of, say, 10, after applying padding, this pair is converted to [PAD, PAD, PAD, PAD, PAD, PAD, "?", "you", "are", "How"].

```python
def pad_sentence_batch(sentence_batch, vocab_to_int):
"""Including <PAD> token in sentence to make all batches of
same length"""
    max_sentence = max([len(sentence) for sentence in sentence_
    batch])
    return [sentence + [vocab_to_int['<PAD>']] * (max_
    sentence - len(sentence)) for sentence in sentence_batch]
```

The following code maps the words in the vocabulary of the newly formed training dataset and assigns a frequency token to each of the words.

```python
# Create a dictionary for the frequency of the vocabulary
vocab = {}
for question in short_questions:
    for word in question.split():
        if word not in vocab:
            vocab[word] = 1
        else:
            vocab[word] += 1

for answer in short_answers:
    for word in answer.split():
        if word not in vocab:
            vocab[word] = 1
        else:
            vocab[word] += 1
```

As with the operations performed in Chapter 2, we will remove the words that have low frequency in the training dataset, as such words that won't introduce any significant information to model.

```python
# Remove rare words from the vocabulary.
threshold = 1
count = 0
for k,v in vocab.items():
    if v >= threshold:
        count += 1

print("Size of total vocab:", len(vocab))
> Size of total vocab: 18983

print("Size of vocab we will use:", count)
> Size of vocab we will use: 18983

# Create dictionaries to provide a unique integer for each
word.
questions_vocab_to_int = {}

word_num = 0
for word, count in vocab.items():
    if count >= threshold:
        questions_vocab_to_int[word] = word_num
        word_num += 1

answers_vocab_to_int = {}

word_num = 0
for word, count in vocab.items():
    if count >= threshold:
        answers_vocab_to_int[word] = word_num
        word_num += 1
```

As there are multiple words or customized symbols being generated by the decoder, we must add new tokens to the present vocabulary of the training dataset and include these in the current dictionary as well. Basic information regarding the four tokens included follows:

- GO: This is the same as the `<start>` token. It is the very first token fed to the decoder, along with the thought vector, to start token generation for the answer.

- EOS: "End of sentence," the same as the `<end>` token that signifies the end of the sentence or completion of an answer. We can't make use of punctuation marks in place of this, as they have totally different meanings with respect to the surrounding context. The EOS token indicates the completion of an answer, as soon as it is generated by the decoder.

- UNK: "Unknown" token. This is used to replace words with much less frequency in the vocabulary, if no additional check/shortlist has been made on the minimum count of occurrence of words. For example, the input sentence `Insurance is highly criticalll1090` will be converted to `Insurance is highly <UNK>`.

- PAD: As the training data is processed in batches of equal length, with all sequences in a batch also being of the same length, the input sentences will be padded with the PAD token on either of the required sides of the sentence. For example, the input sentence `Insurance is highly criticalll1090` will be converted to `Insurance is highly criticalll1090 <PAD> <PAD> <PAD> <PAD>`, for a case in which a maximum length is allowed.

Figure 4-25 displays the usage of the user-defined tokens in the model response (source: http://colah.github.io/). The code to add these tokens follows.

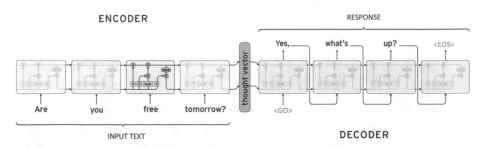

Figure 4-25. *Sample encoder-decoder with usage of tokens*

```
# Adding unique tokens to the present vocabulary
codes = ['<PAD>','<EOS>','<UNK>','<GO>']

for code in codes:
    questions_vocab_to_int[code] = len(questions_vocab_to_
    int)+1

for code in codes:
    answers_vocab_to_int[code] = len(answers_vocab_to_int)+1

# Creating dictionary so as to map the integers to their
respective words, inverse of vocab_to_int
questions_int_to_vocab = {v_i: v for v, v_i in
questions_vocab_to_int.items()}
answers_int_to_vocab = {v_i: v for v, v_i in
answers_vocab_to_int.items()}

print(len(questions_vocab_to_int))
> 18987

print(len(questions_int_to_vocab))
> 18987
```

```
print(len(answers_vocab_to_int))
> 18987
```

```
print(len(answers_int_to_vocab))
> 18987
```

We try to reduce the effective vocabulary size, which will speed up both training and test steps, by simply limiting it to a small number and replacing words outside the vocabulary with a UNK tag. Now, both training and test time can be significantly reduced, but this is obviously not ideal, because we may generate outputs with lots of UNK, but for now, we ensured that the percentage of these tokens is low enough that we won't face any serious issue.

Also, before we feed our data into the model, we must convert every word in the sentence to a unique integer. This can be done by making a vocabulary consisting of all the words and assigning unique numbers to them (one-hot encoded vector).

```
# Convert the text to integers, and replacing any of the words
not present in the respective vocabulary with <UNK> token
questions_int = []
for question in short_questions:
    ints = []
    for word in question.split():
        if word not in questions_vocab_to_int:
            ints.append(questions_vocab_to_int['<UNK>'])
        else:
            ints.append(questions_vocab_to_int[word])
    questions_int.append(ints)

answers_int = []
for answer in short_answers:
    ints = []
```

```
    for word in answer.split():
        if word not in answers_vocab_to_int:
            ints.append(answers_vocab_to_int['<UNK>'])
        else:
            ints.append(answers_vocab_to_int[word])
    answers_int.append(ints)
```

Further check on the count of words being replaced with the <UNK> token. As we have already done the preprocessing step with the removal of the words with low frequency in the vocabulary, none of the words will be replaced by the <UNK> token. It is recommended, however, to include them in a general script.

```
# Calculate what percentage of all words have been replaced
with <UNK>
word_count = 0
unk_count = 0

for question in questions_int:
    for word in question:
        if word == questions_vocab_to_int["<UNK>"]:
            unk_count += 1
        word_count += 1

for answer in answers_int:
    for word in answer:
        if word == answers_vocab_to_int["<UNK>"]:
            unk_count += 1
        word_count += 1

unk_ratio = round(unk_count/word_count,4)*100

print("Total number of words:", word_count)
> Total number of words: 1450824
```

```
print("Number of times <UNK> is used:", unk_count)
> Number of times <UNK> is used: 0

print("Percent of words that are <UNK>: {}%".format(round(unk_
ratio,3)))
> Percent of words that are <UNK>: 0.0%
```

Create ordered sets of the questions and answers on the basis of the number of words in the questions. Sorting the text this way will help in the padding approach we will be using later.

```
# Next, sorting the questions and answers on basis of the
  length of the questions.
# This exercise will reduce the amount of padding being done
  during the training process.
# This will speed up the training process and reduce the
  training loss.

sorted_questions = []
short_questions1 = []
sorted_answers = []
short_answers1= []

for length in range(1, max_line_length+1):
    for i in enumerate(questions_int):
        if len(i[1]) == length:
            sorted_questions.append(questions_int[i[0]])
            short_questions1.append(short_questions[i[0]])
            sorted_answers.append(answers_int[i[0]])
            short_answers1.append(short_answers[i[0]])

print(len(sorted_questions))
> 19108
print(len(sorted_answers))
```

```
> 19108
print(len(short_questions1))
> 19108
print(len(short_answers1))
> 19108
print()

for i in range(3):
    print(sorted_questions[i])
    print(sorted_answers[i])
    print(short_questions1[i])
    print(short_answers1[i])
    print()
```

```
> [219, 13]
[219, 13, 58, 2310, 3636, 1384, 3365... ]
```

why can
why can a simple question but yet so complex why can someone
do this or why can someone do that i have often pondered for
hours to come up with the answer and i believe after years of
thoughtprovoking consultation with friends and relativesi have
the answer to the question why can the answer why not

```
[133, 479, 56]
[242, 4123, 3646, 282, 306, 56, ... ]
```

who governs annuities
if youre asking about all annuities then here are two governing
bodies for variable annuities finra and the department of
insurance variable products like variable annuities are registered
products and come under the oversight of finras jurisdiction but
because it is an annuity insurance product as well it falls under
the department of insurance non finra annuities are governed by
the department of insurance in each state

```
[0, 201, 56]
[29, 202, 6, 29, 10, 3602, 58, 36, ... ]
```

what are annuities

an annuity is an insurance product a life insurance policy
protects you from dying too soon an annuity protects you from
living too long annuities are complex basically in exchange for
a sum of money either immediate or in installments the company
will pay the annuitant a specific amount normally monthly for
the life of the annuitant there are many modifications of this
basic form annuities are taxed differently from other programs

Check a random question answer from the sorted pairs.

```
print(sorted_questions[1547])
> [37, 6, 36, 10, 466]
```

```
print(short_questions1[1547])
> how is life insurance used
```

```
print(sorted_answers[1547])
> [8, 36, 10, 6, 466, 26, 626, 58, 199, 200, 1130, 58, 3512,
31, 105, 208, 601, 10, 6, 466, 26, 626, ...
```

```
print(short_answers1[1547])
> term life insurance is used to provide a death benefit
```
during a specified period of time permanent insurance is used
to provide a death benefit at any time the policy is in force
in order to accomplish this and have level premiums policies
accumulate extra funds these funds are designed to allow the
policy to meet its lifelong obligations however these funds
accumulate tax free and give the policy the potential of
solving many problems from funding education to providing long
term care

Now is the time to define the helper functions that will be used by the seq2seq model. A few of these functions have been drawn from the GitHub code repository (https://github.com/Currie32/Chatbot-from-Movie-Dialogue), which has a similar application.

Define the function to create placeholders for our model's inputs.

```
def model_inputs():
    input_data = tf.placeholder(tf.int32, [None, None],
    name='input')
    targets = tf.placeholder(tf.int32, [None, None],
    name='targets')
    lr = tf.placeholder(tf.float32, name='learning_rate')
    keep_prob = tf.placeholder(tf.float32, name='keep_prob')
    return input_data, targets, lr, keep_prob
```

Delete the last word ID in each of the batches and append the <GO> token at the start of each of the batches.

```
def process_encoding_input(target_data, vocab_to_int, batch_
size):

    ending = tf.strided_slice(target_data, [0, 0],
    [batch_size, -1], [1, 1])
    dec_input = tf.concat([tf.fill([batch_size, 1], vocab_to_
    int['<GO>']), ending], 1)

    return dec_input
```

The normal RNN takes care of past states (preserves them into a memory), but what if you want to somehow include future also into the context. By using bidirectional RNNs, we can connect two hidden layers of opposite directions to the same output. By this structure, the output layer can get information from past and future states.

Thus, we define the encoding layer of the seq2seq model with LSTM cells and a bidirectional encoder. The encoder layer's state, i.e., weights, is taken as an input to the decoding layer.

```
def encoding_layer(rnn_inputs, rnn_size, num_layers, keep_prob,
sequence_length):
    lstm = tf.contrib.rnn.BasicLSTMCell(rnn_size)
    drop = tf.contrib.rnn.DropoutWrapper(lstm, input_keep_prob
    = keep_prob)
    enc_cell = tf.contrib.rnn.MultiRNNCell([drop] * num_layers)
    _, enc_state = tf.nn.bidirectional_dynamic_rnn(cell_fw =
    enc_cell, cell_bw = enc_cell, sequence_length = sequence_
    length, inputs = rnn_inputs, dtype=tf.float32)
    return enc_state
```

The attention mechanism, explained in Chapter 3, has been used. This will reduce the generated loss significantly. The attention states are set to 0, to maximize the model performance, and for the attention mechanism, a lesser expensive Bahdanau attention is used. Refer to the paper "Effective Approaches to Attention-based Neural Machine Translation" (https://arxiv.org/pdf/1508.04025.pdf) for a comparison of the Luong and Bahdanau attention techniques.

```
def decoding_layer_train(encoder_state, dec_cell, dec_embed_
input, sequence_length, decoding_scope, output_fn, keep_prob,
batch_size):

    attention_states = tf.zeros([batch_size, 1, dec_cell.
    output_size])

    att_keys, att_vals, att_score_fn, att_construct_fn =
    tf.contrib.seq2seq.prepare_attention(attention_states,
    attention_option="bahdanau", num_units=dec_cell.output_size)
```

```
train_decoder_fn = tf.contrib.seq2seq.attention_decoder_fn_
train(encoder_state[0], att_keys, att_vals,  att_score_fn,
att_construct_fn,  name = "attn_dec_train")

train_pred, _, _ = tf.contrib.seq2seq.dynamic_rnn_
decoder(dec_cell, train_decoder_fn,  dec_embed_input,
sequence_length, scope=decoding_scope)
train_pred_drop = tf.nn.dropout(train_pred, keep_prob)

return output_fn(train_pred_drop)
```

The decoding_layer_infer() function creates the proper responses to the queried questions. The function makes use of the additional attention parameters, to predict the words in the answers, and it is not coupled with any dropout, as during the final scoring phase. Here, while generating answers, dropout is not taken into consideration, so as to make use of all the neurons present across the network.

```
def decoding_layer_infer(encoder_state, dec_cell, dec_
embeddings, start_of_sequence_id, end_of_sequence_id,
                         maximum_length, vocab_size, decoding_
                         scope, output_fn, keep_prob, batch_
                         size):

    attention_states = tf.zeros([batch_size, 1, dec_cell.
    output_size])

    att_keys, att_vals, att_score_fn, att_construct_fn =
    tf.contrib.seq2seq.prepare_attention(attention_states,
    attention_option="bahdanau", num_units=dec_cell.output_
    size)
```

```
infer_decoder_fn = tf.contrib.seq2seq.attention_decoder_
fn_inference(output_fn, encoder_state[0], att_keys, att_
vals, att_score_fn, att_construct_fn,
                        dec_embeddings, start_of_sequence_id,
                        end_of_sequence_id, maximum_length,
                        vocab_size, name = "attn_dec_inf")

infer_logits, _, _ = tf.contrib.seq2seq.dynamic_rnn_
decoder(dec_cell, infer_decoder_fn, scope=decoding_scope)`


return infer_logits
```

The decoding_layer() function creates the inference and training logits and initializes the weights and biases with the given standard deviation, using the truncated normal distribution.

```
def decoding_layer(dec_embed_input, dec_embeddings, encoder_
state, vocab_size, sequence_length, rnn_size,
                    num_layers, vocab_to_int, keep_prob, batch_
                    size):
    with tf.variable_scope("decoding") as decoding_scope:
        lstm = tf.contrib.rnn.BasicLSTMCell(rnn_size)
        drop = tf.contrib.rnn.DropoutWrapper(lstm, input_keep_
        prob = keep_prob)
        dec_cell = tf.contrib.rnn.MultiRNNCell([drop] * num_
        layers)

        weights = tf.truncated_normal_initializer(stddev=0.1)
        biases = tf.zeros_initializer()
        output_fn = lambda x: tf.contrib.layers.fully_
        connected(x, vocab_size, None, scope=decoding_scope,
        weights_initializer = weights, biases_initializer =
        biases)
```

```
        train_logits = decoding_layer_train(encoder_state,
        dec_cell,  dec_embed_input, sequence_length,  decoding_
        scope, output_fn, keep_prob, batch_size)

        decoding_scope.reuse_variables()
        infer_logits = decoding_layer_infer(encoder_state,
        dec_cell, dec_embeddings, vocab_to_int['<GO>'], vocab_
        to_int['<EOS>'],
                        sequence_length - 1, vocab_size,  decoding_
                        scope, output_fn, keep_prob, batch_size)

    return train_logits, infer_logits
```

The seq2seq_model() function has been used to put all the previously
defined functions together and also to initialize the embeddings using
random uniform distribution. The function will be used in the final graph
to compute the training and inference logits.

```
def seq2seq_model(input_data, target_data, keep_prob, batch_
size, sequence_length, answers_vocab_size,
                    questions_vocab_size, enc_embedding_size,
                    dec_embedding_size, rnn_size, num_layers,
                    questions_vocab_to_int):
    enc_embed_input = tf.contrib.layers.embed_sequence(input_
    data, answers_vocab_size+1,  enc_embedding_size,
    initializer = tf.random_uniform_initializer(0,1))

    enc_state = encoding_layer(enc_embed_input, rnn_size,
    num_layers, keep_prob, sequence_length)

    dec_input = process_encoding_input(target_data,
    questions_vocab_to_int, batch_size)
```

```
dec_embeddings = tf.Variable(tf.random_uniform([questions_
vocab_size+1, dec_embedding_size], 0, 1))
dec_embed_input = tf.nn.embedding_lookup(dec_embeddings,
dec_input)

train_logits, infer_logits = decoding_layer(dec_embed_
input, dec_embeddings, enc_state, questions_vocab_size,
                        sequence_length, rnn_size,
                        num_layers, questions_vocab_to_
                        int,  keep_prob, batch_size)

return train_logits, infer_logits
```

When the total number of training instances (N) is large, a small number of training instances (B<<N), which constitute a batch, can be used in one iteration, to estimate the gradient of the loss function and update the parameters of the network.

Note   It takes n (=N/B) iterations to use the entire training data once. This constitutes an *epoch*. So, the total number of times the parameters get updated is (N/B)*E, where E is the number of epochs.

Finally, we have defined our seq2seq model that will take the encoding and decoding part and train them simultaneously. Now, set the following model parameters and start the session for optimization.

- **Epoch**: A single pass through the entire training set

- **Batch size**: Simultaneous number of sentences in input

- **Rnn_size**: Number of nodes in hidden layer

- **Num_layers**: Number of hidden layers

- **Embedding size**: Embedding dimension

- **Learning rate**: How quickly a network abandons old beliefs for new ones

- **Keep probability**: Used to control the dropout. Dropout is a simple technique to prevent over-fitting. It essentially drops some of the unit activations in a layer, by making them zero.

```
# Setting the model parameters
epochs = 50
batch_size = 64
rnn_size = 512
num_layers = 2
encoding_embedding_size = 512
decoding_embedding_size = 512
learning_rate = 0.005
learning_rate_decay = 0.9
min_learning_rate = 0.0001
keep_probability = 0.75

tf.reset_default_graph()
# Starting the session
sess = tf.InteractiveSession()

# Loading the model inputs
input_data, targets, lr, keep_prob = model_inputs()

# Sequence length is max_line_length for each batch
sequence_length = tf.placeholder_with_default(max_line_length,
None, name='sequence_length')

# Finding shape of the input data for sequence_loss
input_shape = tf.shape(input_data)

# Create the training and inference logits
```

```
train_logits, inference_logits = seq2seq_model(
tf.reverse(input_data, [-1]), targets, keep_prob, batch_size,
sequence_length, len(answers_vocab_to_int),
    len(questions_vocab_to_int), encoding_embedding_size,
decoding_embedding_size, rnn_size, num_layers,  questions_
vocab_to_int)
```

```
# Create inference logits tensor
tf.identity(inference_logits, 'logits')
```

```
with tf.name_scope("optimization"):
    # Calculating Loss function
    cost = tf.contrib.seq2seq.sequence_loss( train_logits,
    targets, tf.ones([input_shape[0], sequence_length]))

    # Using Adam Optimizer
    optimizer = tf.train.AdamOptimizer(learning_rate)

    # Performing Gradient Clipping to handle the vanishing
    gradient problem
    gradients = optimizer.compute_gradients(cost)
    capped_gradients = [(tf.clip_by_value(grad, -5., 5.), var)
    for grad, var in gradients if grad is not None]
    train_op = optimizer.apply_gradients(capped_gradients)
```

The batch_data() function helps to create batches for both questions and answers.

```
def batch_data(questions, answers, batch_size):

    for batch_i in range(0, len(questions)//batch_size):
        start_i = batch_i * batch_size
        questions_batch = questions[start_i:start_i + batch_
        size]
```

```
        answers_batch = answers[start_i:start_i + batch_size]
        pad_questions_batch = np.array(pad_sentence_
        batch(questions_batch, questions_vocab_to_int))
        pad_answers_batch = np.array(pad_sentence_
        batch(answers_batch, answers_vocab_to_int))
        yield pad_questions_batch, pad_answers_batch
```

Hold 15 percent of the total dataset for validation, and rest 85 percent to train the model.

```
# Creating train and validation datasets for both questions and
answers, with 15% to validation
train_valid_split = int(len(sorted_questions)*0.15)

train_questions = sorted_questions[train_valid_split:]
train_answers = sorted_answers[train_valid_split:]

valid_questions = sorted_questions[:train_valid_split]
valid_answers = sorted_answers[:train_valid_split]

print(len(train_questions))
print(len(valid_questions))
```

Set the training parameters and initializing the declared variables.

```
display_step = 20          # Check training loss after every 20
                             batches

stop_early = 0

stop = 5                     # If the validation loss decreases after
                             5 consecutive checks, stop training

validation_check = ((len(train_questions))//batch_size//2)-
1          # Counter for checking validation loss

total_train_loss = 0      # Record the training loss for each
                             display step
```

```python
summary_valid_loss = []      # Record the validation loss for
                             #   saving improvements in the model

checkpoint= "./best_model.ckpt"    # creating the checkpoint
                                   #   file in the current
                                   #   directory

sess.run(tf.global_variables_initializer())
```

Train the model.

```python
for epoch_i in range(1, epochs+1):
    for batch_i, (questions_batch, answers_batch) in enumerate(
            batch_data(train_questions, train_answers, batch_
            size)):
        start_time = time.time()
        _, loss = sess.run(
            [train_op, cost],
            {input_data: questions_batch, targets: answers_
            batch,  lr: learning_rate,
             sequence_length: answers_batch.shape[1], keep_
            prob: keep_probability})

        total_train_loss += loss
        end_time = time.time()
        batch_time = end_time - start_time

        if batch_i % display_step == 0:
            print('Epoch {:>3}/{} Batch {:>4}/{} - Loss:
            {:>6.3f}, Seconds: {:>4.2f}'
                    .format(epoch_i, epochs, batch_i,
                            len(train_questions) // batch_size,
                            total_train_loss / display_step,
                            batch_time*display_step))
            total_train_loss = 0
```

```
if batch_i % validation_check == 0 and batch_i > 0:
    total_valid_loss = 0
    start_time = time.time()
    for batch_ii, (questions_batch, answers_batch)
    in enumerate(batch_data(valid_questions, valid_
    answers, batch_size)):
        valid_loss = sess.run(
        cost, {input_data: questions_batch, targets:
        answers_batch, lr: learning_rate,
                sequence_length: answers_batch.shape[1],
                keep_prob: 1})
        total_valid_loss += valid_loss
    end_time = time.time()
    batch_time = end_time - start_time
    avg_valid_loss = total_valid_loss / (len(valid_
    questions) / batch_size)
    print('Valid Loss: {:>6.3f}, Seconds: {:>5.2f}'.
    format(avg_valid_loss, batch_time))

    # Reduce learning rate, but not below its minimum
    value
    learning_rate *= learning_rate_decay
    if learning_rate < min_learning_rate:
        learning_rate = min_learning_rate

    summary_valid_loss.append(avg_valid_loss)
    if avg_valid_loss <= min(summary_valid_loss):
        print('New Record!')
        stop_early = 0
        saver = tf.train.Saver()
        saver.save(sess, checkpoint)
```

```
        else:
            print("No Improvement.")
            stop_early += 1
            if stop_early == stop:
                break

    if stop_early == stop:
        print("Stopping Training.")
        break
```

```
> Epoch   1/50 Batch     0/253 - Loss:  0.494, Seconds: 1060.06
> Epoch   1/50 Batch    20/253 - Loss:  8.450, Seconds: 905.71
> Epoch   1/50 Batch    40/253 - Loss:  4.540, Seconds: 933.88
> Epoch   1/50 Batch    60/253 - Loss:  4.401, Seconds: 740.15
> Epoch   1/50 Batch    80/253 - Loss:  4.453, Seconds: 831.04
> Epoch   1/50 Batch   100/253 - Loss:  4.338, Seconds: 774.67
> Epoch   1/50 Batch   120/253 - Loss:  4.295, Seconds: 832.49
Valid Loss:  4.091, Seconds: 675.05
New Record!
> Epoch   1/50 Batch   140/253 - Loss:  4.255, Seconds: 822.40
> Epoch   1/50 Batch   160/253 - Loss:  4.232, Seconds: 888.85
> Epoch   1/50 Batch   180/253 - Loss:  4.168, Seconds: 858.95
> Epoch   1/50 Batch   200/253 - Loss:  4.093, Seconds: 849.23
> Epoch   1/50 Batch   220/253 - Loss:  4.034, Seconds: 846.77
> Epoch   1/50 Batch   240/253 - Loss:  4.005, Seconds: 809.77
Valid Loss:  3.903, Seconds: 509.83
New Record!
...
...
...
...
...
```

Define the question_to_seq() function to take the input question either from the user, or pick a random question from the dataset and convert it to the integer format to be used by the model.

```
def question_to_seq(question, vocab_to_int):
    """Creating the question to be taken as input by the model"""
    question = clean_text(question)
    return [vocab_to_int.get(word, vocab_to_int['<UNK>']) for
    word in question.split()]
```

Now is the time to get fruits from the tree planted at the start of this section. So, here we will check the output of our seq2seq model by giving a random question as input. The answer will be generated by the trained model.

```
# Selecting a random question from the full lot
random = np.random.choice(len(short_questions))
input_question = short_questions[random]
print(input_question)
```

```
> what exactly does adjustable life insurance mean
```

```
# Transforming the selected question in the desired format of
IDs and Words
input_question = question_to_seq(input_question, questions_
vocab_to_int)
```

```
# Applying Padding to the question to reach the max_line_length
input_question = input_question + [questions_vocab_to_
int["<PAD>"]] * (max_line_length - len(input_question))
```

```
# Correcting the shape of input_data, by adding the empty questions
batch_shell = np.zeros((batch_size, max_line_length))
```

```
# Setting the input question as the first question
batch_shell[0] = input_question
```

```
# Passing  input question to the model
answer_logits = sess.run(inference_logits, {input_data: batch_
shell, keep_prob: 1.0})[0]
```

```
# Removing padding from Question and Answer both
pad_q = questions_vocab_to_int["<PAD>"]
pad_a = answers_vocab_to_int["<PAD>"]
```

```
# Printing the final Answer output by the model
print('Question')
print('Word Ids: {}'.format([i for i in input_question if i !=
pad_q]))
print('Input Words: {}'.format([questions_int_to_vocab[i] for i
in input_question if i != pad_q]))
print('\n')
```

```
> Question
```

```
> Word Ids: [17288, 16123, 9831, 13347, 1694, 11205, 7655]
```

```
> Input Words: ['what', 'exactly', 'does', 'adjustable',
'life', 'insurance', 'mean']
```

```
print('\nAnswer')
print('Word Ids: {}'.format([i for i in np.argmax(answer_
logits, 1) if i != pad_a]))
```

```
print('Response Words: {}'.format([answers_int_to_vocab[i] for
i in np.argmax(answer_logits, 1) if i != pad_a]))
```

```
print('\n')
```

```
print(' '.join(([questions_int_to_vocab[i] for i in input_
question if i != pad_q])))
```

```
print(' '.join(([answers_int_to_vocab[i] for i in
np.argmax(answer_logits, 1) if i != pad_a])))
```

> Answer

> Word Ids: [10130, 10344, 13123, 2313, 1133, 1694,
11205, 6968, 966, 10130, 3030, 2313, 5964, 10561, 10130, 9158,
17702, 13344, 13278, 10130, 7457, 14167, 17931, 14479, 10130,
6968, 9158, 8521, 10130, 9158, 17702, 12230, 10130, 6968, 8679,
1688, 10130, 7457, 14167, 17931, 9472, 10130, 9158, 12230,
10130, 6968, 8679, 1688, 10130, 7457, 14167, 17931, 18293,
10130, 16405, 16640, 6396, 3613, 2313, 10130, 6968, 10130,
6968, 8679, 1688, 10130, 7457, 14167, 17931, 18293, 10130,
16405, 16640, 6396, 3613, 10628, 13040, 10130, 6968]

> Response Words: ['the', 'face', 'value', 'of', 'a', 'life',
'insurance', 'policy', 'is', 'the', 'amount', 'of', 'time',
'that', 'the', 'insured', 'person', 'passes', 'with', 'the',
'death', 'benefit', 'proceeds', 'from', 'the', 'policy',
'insured', 'if', 'the', 'insured', 'person', 'dies', 'the',
'policy', 'will', 'pay', 'the', 'death', 'benefit', 'proceeds',
'whenever', 'the', 'insured', 'dies', 'the', 'policy', 'will',
'pay', 'the', 'death', 'benefit', 'proceeds', 'within', 'the',
'two', 'year', 'contestability', 'period', 'of', 'the',
'policy', 'the', 'policy', 'will', 'pay', 'the', 'death',
'benefit', 'proceeds', 'within', 'the', 'two', 'year',
'contestability', 'period', 'specified', 'in', 'the', 'policy']

> what exactly does adjustable life insurance mean

> the face value of a life insurance policy is the amount of
time that the insured person passes with the death benefit

proceeds from the policy insured if the insured person dies
the policy will pay the death benefit proceeds whenever the
insured dies the policy will pay the death benefit proceeds
within the two year contestability period of the policy the
policy will pay the death benefit proceeds within the two year
contestability period specified in the policy

The last paragraph is the output of the question "What exactly does adjustable life insurance mean?" that we have put into the model. Well, it does not sound grammatically correct, but that is a whole different issue that could be dealt in a better way by training the model with more datasets and refined embeddings.

Assuming there is no major update happening in the conversation text over time, one can make use of the trained model object and imbibe it in the chatbot application, to produce beautiful replies to the questions posed by the end user of the chatbot. This has been left as an exercise for the reader. Enjoy conversing with your own chatbot! For additional fun, you can try training the model on personal chats with your friends, to see whether your chatbot is able to resemble of your loved ones successfully or not. Now you know that all that is needed is the conversation text file of two persons to create a fully functional chatbot.

Next Steps

This chapter made use of the concepts explained in Chapter 3 and helped in making a chatbot and training a text-generating model that can be further embedded to the Facebook Messenger chatbot. In Chapter 5, we will present an implementation of the sentiment classification taken from a paper released at the 5th International Conference on Learning Representations (ICLR 2017). We recommend that our readers replicate the examples in the chapter and explore different use cases of text generation techniques on the diverse set of available public datasets.

Research Paper Implementation: Sentiment Classification

Chapter 5 concludes this book with the implementation of sentiment analysis from a research paper. The first section of this chapter details the approach mentioned, followed by a second section devoted to its implementation, using TensorFlow. To ensure there is a difference between the actual paper we used and our results, we have selected a different dataset for test purposes, so the accuracy of our results may vary from those presented in the actual research paper.

The dataset being used is available for public use and is included as a sample dataset in the Keras library. This chapter links the theories and practical examples shared in Chapters 2 and 3 and creates an additional layer, by using the modeling approaches followed in the research paper.

Our implementation exercise owes its success to the paper "A Structured Self-attentive Sentence Embedding" (https://arxiv.org/pdf/1703.03130.pdf), presented at ICLR 2017 (5th International Conference on Learning Representations) by a team of research scientists

© Palash Goyal, Sumit Pandey, Karan Jain 2018
P. Goyal, et al., *Deep Learning for Natural Language Processing*,
https://doi.org/10.1007/978-1-4842-3685-7_5

from IBM Watson and the Montreal Institute for Learning Algorithms (MILA) of the University of Montreal (Université de Montréal) and subsequently published.

The paper suggests a new modeling technique to extract an interpretable sentence embedding, by introducing a self-attention mechanism. The model uses a two-dimensional matrix to represent the sentence embedding, in place of a vector, in which each of the matrices represents a different segment of the sentence. In addition, a self-attention mechanism and a unique regularization term are proposed. The embedding method proposed can be visualized easily, to figure out what specific parts of the sentence ultimately are being encoded into the sentence embedding. The research conducted shares the performance evaluation of the proposed model on three different types of tasks.

- Author profiling

- Sentiment classification

- Textual entailment

The model has turned out to be quite promising, compared to other current sentence-embedding techniques, for all three of the preceding types of tasks.

Self-Attentive Sentence Embedding

Various supervised and unsupervised sentence-embedding models have been proposed previously, such as skip-thought vectors, paragraph vectors, recursive autoencoders, sequential denoising autoencoders, FastSent, etc., but the proposed method in the paper concerned uses a new self-attention mechanism that allows it to extract different aspects of the sentence into multiple vector representations. The matrix structure, with the penalization term, gives the model a greater capacity to disentangle the latent information from the input sentence.

Moreover, the linguistic structures are not used to guide the sentence representation model. Additionally, using this method, one can easily create visualizations that help in the interpretation of the learned representations.

The *skip-thought vector* is an unsupervised learning of a generic distributed sentence encoder. Using the continuity of text from books, an encoder-decoder model is trained to attempt to reconstruct the surrounding sentences of an encoded passage. Sentences that share semantic and syntactic properties are thus mapped to similar vector representations. For further information related to this, refer to the original paper, available at https://arxiv.org/abs/1506.06726.

A *paragraph vector* is an unsupervised algorithm that learns fixed-length feature representations from variable-length pieces of texts, such as sentences, paragraphs, and documents. The algorithm represents each document by a dense vector that is trained to predict words in the document. Empirical results presented in the paper show that paragraph vectors outperform bag-of-words models, as well as other techniques for text representations. A more detailed explanation on this is included in the original research paper, available at https://arxiv.org/abs/1405.4053.

Figure 5-1 shows a sample model structure used to showcase the sentence-embedding model when combined with a fully connected and softmax layer for sentiment analysis.

Note   Blue shapes stand for hidden representations, and red shapes stand for weights, annotations, or input/output.

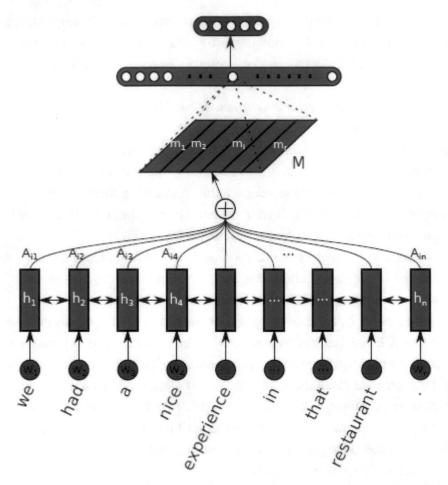

Figure 5-1. *The sentence-embedding model is computed as multiple weighted sums of hidden states from a bidirectional long short-term memory (LSTM) ($h_1, ..., h_n$)*

Proposed Approach

This section covers the proposed self-attentive sentence-embedding model and the regularization term proposed for it. Both concepts are explained in separate subsections and are like those mentioned in the actual paper. The reader has the option of referring to the original paper for additional information, although the content presented in this section is sufficient for a general understanding of the proposed approaches.

The proposed attention mechanism is only performed once, and it focuses directly on the semantics that make sense for discriminating the targets. It is less focused on relations between words, but more so on the semantics of the whole sentence that each word contributes to. Computation-wise, the method scales up well with the sentence length, as it doesn't require the LSTM to compute an annotation vector over all its previous words.

Model

The proposed sentence-embedding model in "A Structured Self-attentive Sentence Embedding" consists of two parts:

- **Bidirectional LSTM**

- **Self-attention mechanism**

The self-attention mechanism provides a set of summation weight vectors for the LSTM hidden states (Figure 5-2).

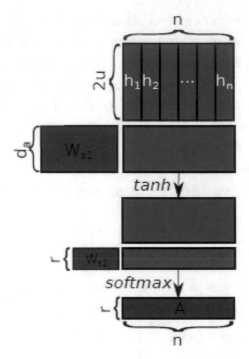

Figure 5-2. *The summation weights (A_{i1}, ..., A_{in}) are computed as illustrated*

The set of summation weight vectors is dotted with the LSTM hidden states, and the resulting weighted LSTM hidden states are considered as an embedding for the sentence. It can be combined with, for example, a multilayer perceptron (MLP), to be applied on a downstream application. The figures shown belong to an example in which the proposed sentence-embedding model is applied to sentiment analysis, combined with a fully connected layer and a softmax layer.

Note   For the sentiment analysis exercise, the figures used in the preceding illustration will be sufficient to describe the desired model.

(*Optional*)   In addition to using a fully connected layer, an approach that prunes weight connections by utilizing the two-dimensional structure of matrix sentence embedding has also been proposed in the paper and has been detailed in its Appendix A.

Suppose we have a sentence that has n tokens, represented in a sequence of word embeddings.

$$S = \left(w_1, w_2, \ldots, w_n \right)$$

Here, w_i is a vector standing for a d dimensional word embedding for the i-th word in the sentence. S is thus a sequence represented as a two-dimensional matrix, which concatenates all the word embeddings together. S should have the shape n-by-d.

Now, each entry in the sequence S is independent of the other. To gain some dependency between adjacent words within a single sentence, we use a bidirectional LSTM to process the sentence

$$\overrightarrow{h_t} = \overrightarrow{LSTM}\left(w_t, \overrightarrow{h_{(t-1)}} \right)$$

$$\overleftarrow{h_t} = \overleftarrow{LSTM}\left(w_t, \overleftarrow{h_{(t+1)}} \right)$$

We then concatenate each $\overrightarrow{h_t}$ with $\overleftarrow{h_t}$, to obtain a hidden state h_t. Let the hidden unit number for each unidirectional LSTM be u. For simplicity, we note all the n h_ts as H, which have the size n-by-$2u$.

$$H = (h_1, h_2, \ldots, h_n)$$

Our aim is to encode a variable-length sentence into a fixed-size embedding. We achieve that by choosing a linear combination of the n LSTM hidden vectors in H. Computing the linear combination requires the self-attention mechanism. The attention mechanism takes all of the LSTM hidden states H as input and outputs a vector of weights a, as follows:

$$a = softmax\left(\mathbf{W}_{s2} \, tanh\left(w_{s1} H^T\right)\right)$$

Here, W_{s1} is a weight matrix with a shape of d_a-by-$2u$, and W_{s2} is a vector of parameters with size d_a, where d_a is a hyperparameter we can set arbitrarily. Because H is sized n-by-$2u$, the annotation vector a will have a size n. The *softmax()* ensures all the computed weights add up to 1. We then add up the LSTM hidden states H according to the weights provided by a, to get a vector representation **m** of the input sentence.

This vector representation usually focuses on a specific component of the sentence, such as a special set of related words or phrases. So, it is expected to reflect an aspect, or component, of the semantics in a sentence. However, there can be multiple components in a sentence that together form the overall semantics of it, especially for long sentences. (For example, two clauses linked together by an "and") Thus, to represent the overall semantics of the sentence, we need multiple **m**'s that focus on different parts of the sentence. Thus, we must perform multiple hops of attention. Say we want r different parts to be extracted from the sentence. For this, we extend the W_{s2} into an r-by-d_a matrix, note it as W_{s2}, and the resulting annotation vector a becomes annotation matrix A.

Formally,

$$A = softmax\left(W_{s2} \, tanh\left(W_{s1} H^T\right)\right)$$

Here, the *softmax()* is performed along the second dimension of its input. We can deem the preceding equation as a two-layer MLP without bias, whose hidden unit numbers is d_a, and whose parameters are $\{W_{s2}, W_{s1}\}$.

The embedding vector **m** then becomes an r-by-$2u$ embedding matrix M. We compute the r weighted sums by multiplying the annotation matrix A and LSTM hidden states H. The resulting matrix is the sentence embedding:

$$M = A\,H$$

Penalization Term

The embedding matrix M can suffer from redundancy problems, if the attention mechanism always provides similar summation weights for all the r hops. Thus, we need a penalization term, to encourage the diversity of summation weight vectors across different hops of attention.

The best way to evaluate the diversity is definitely the *Kullback Leibler divergence* (KL) between any two of the summation weight vectors.

KL divergence is used to measure the difference between two probability distributions over the same variable x. It is related to cross entropy and information divergence. For the given two probability distributions, $p(x)$ and $q(x)$, KL divergence serves as a nonsymmetric measure of the divergence of $q(x)$ from $p(x)$, is denoted as $D_{KL}(p(x), q(x))$, and is a measure of the information lost when $q(x)$ is used to approximate $p(x)$.

For a discrete random variable x, if $p(x)$ and $q(x)$ are its two probability distributions, then both $p(x)$ and $q(x)$ add up to 1, and $p(x) > 0$ and $q(x) > 0$ for any x in X.

$$D_{KL}\left(p(x), q(x)\right) = \sum_{x \in X} p(x)\ln\frac{p(x)}{q(x)}$$

where,

$$D_{KL}\left(p(x), q(x)\right) \geq 0,$$

$$D_{KL}\left(P \| Q\right) = 0, \text{ if and only if, } P = Q$$

The KL divergence measures the expected number of extra bits required to code samples from $p(x)$ when using a code based on $q(x)$, rather than using a code based on $p(x)$. Usually, $p(x)$ represents the "actual" data distribution of observations, or a precisely calculated theoretical distribution, and $q(x)$ represents a theory, or model, or approximation of $p(x)$. Similar to the discrete version, KL divergence holds continuous version as well.

KL divergence is not a distance measure, even though it measures the "distance" between two distributions, as it is not a metric measure. Moreover, it is not symmetric in nature, i.e., the KL divergence value from $p(x)$ to $q(x)$ is not the same as the KL divergence value from $q(x)$ to $p(x)$, in most of cases. Also, it might not satisfy the triangular inequality.

However, that is not very stable in this case, as, here, maximization of a set of KL divergence is being tried (instead of minimizing only one, which is the usual case), and as optimization of the annotation matrix A is performed, to have a lot of sufficiently small or even zero values at different softmax output units, the vast amount of zeros makes the training unstable. There is another feature that KL divergence doesn't provide and is the need of the hour, which is each individual row to focus on a single aspect of semantics. This requires the probability mass in the annotation softmax output to be more focused, but with a KL divergence penalty, it won't serve the purpose.

Thus, a new penalization term is introduced that overcomes the previously mentioned shortcomings. Compared to the KL divergence penalization, this term consumes only one-third of the computation. The dot product of A and its transpose are used, subtracted from an identity matrix, as a measure of redundancy.

$$P = \left\| \left(AA^T - I \right) \right\|_F^2$$

In the preceding equation, $\| \circ \|_F^2$ stands for the *Frobenius* norm of a matrix. Like adding an L2 regularization term, this penalization term, P, will be multiplied by a coefficient, and we minimize it, together with the original loss, which is dependent on the downstream application.

Let's consider two different summation vectors, a^i and a^j, in A. Because of softmax, all entries within any summation vector in A should add up to 1. Thus, they can be deemed as probability masses in a discrete probability distribution. For any non-diagonal elements a_{ij} $(i \neq j)$ in the $A.A^T$ matrix, it corresponds to a summation over the element-wise product of two distributions:

$$0 < a_{ij} = \sum_{k=1}^{n} a_k^i a_k^j < 1$$

Where a_k^i and a_k^j are the k-th element in the a^i and a^j vectors, respectively. In the most extreme case, where there is no overlap between the two probability distributions a^i and a^j, the corresponding a_{ij} will be 0 otherwise it will have a positive value. On the other extreme end, if the two distributions are identical, and all concentrate on one single word, it will have a maximum value of 1. We subtract an identity matrix from $A.A^T$, which forces the elements on the diagonal of $A.A^T$ to approximate 1, which encourages each summation vector a^i to focus on as few numbers of words as possible, forcing each vector to be focused on a single aspect, and all other elements to 0, which punishes redundancy between different summation vectors.

Visualization

The General case visualization presents the results of the *Author Profiling* task and shows the two types of visualization being used. The second case, on sentiment analysis, makes use of the second means of visualization, for a heatmap of reviews on Yelp.

General Case

The interpretation of the sentence embedding is quite straightforward, because of the existence of annotation matrix A. For each row in the sentence embedding matrix M, its corresponding annotation vector a_i is present. Each element in this vector corresponds to how much contribution the LSTM hidden state of a token on that position contributes to. Thus, a heatmap could be drawn for each row of the embedding matrix M.

This method of visualization hints at what is encoded in each part of the embedding, adding an extra layer of interpretation. Figure 5-3 shows heat maps for two models trained on the Twitter Age dataset (`http://pan.webis.de/clef16/pan16-web/author-profiling.html`).

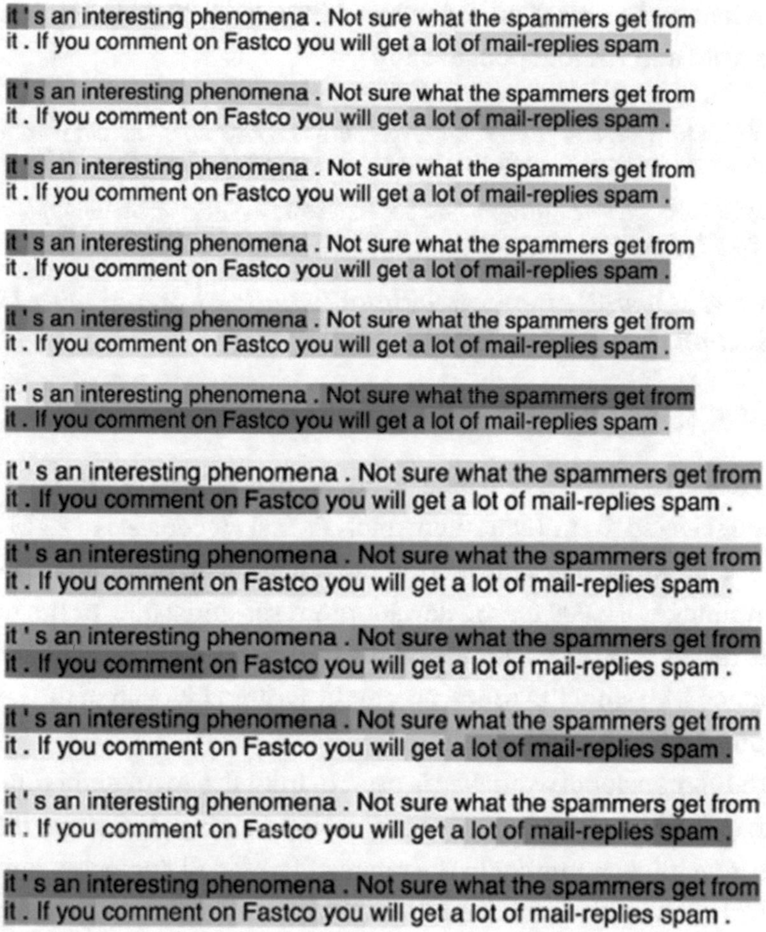

it's an interesting phenomena . Not sure what the spammers get from it . If you comment on Fastco you will get a lot of mail-replies spam .

it's an interesting phenomena . Not sure what the spammers get from it . If you comment on Fastco you will get a lot of mail-replies spam .

it's an interesting phenomena . Not sure what the spammers get from it . If you comment on Fastco you will get a lot of mail-replies spam .

it's an interesting phenomena . Not sure what the spammers get from it . If you comment on Fastco you will get a lot of mail-replies spam .

it's an interesting phenomena . Not sure what the spammers get from it . If you comment on Fastco you will get a lot of mail-replies spam .

it's an interesting phenomena . Not sure what the spammers get from it . If you comment on Fastco you will get a lot of mail-replies spam .

it's an interesting phenomena . Not sure what the spammers get from it . If you comment on Fastco you will get a lot of mail-replies spam .

it's an interesting phenomena . Not sure what the spammers get from it . If you comment on Fastco you will get a lot of mail-replies spam .

it's an interesting phenomena . Not sure what the spammers get from it . If you comment on Fastco you will get a lot of mail-replies spam .

it's an interesting phenomena . Not sure what the spammers get from it . If you comment on Fastco you will get a lot of mail-replies spam .

it's an interesting phenomena . Not sure what the spammers get from it . If you comment on Fastco you will get a lot of mail-replies spam .

it's an interesting phenomena . Not sure what the spammers get from it . If you comment on Fastco you will get a lot of mail-replies spam .

Figure 5-3. *Heatmaps of six random detailed attentions from 30 rows of matrix embedding, and for two models without and with 1.0 penalization*

The second means of visualization can be achieved by adding up the overall annotation vectors and then normalizing the resulting weight vector to add up to 1. Because it adds up all aspects of semantics of a sentence, it yields a general view of what the embedding mostly focuses on. One can figure out which words the embedding takes into account the most and which are skipped by the embedding. Figure 5-4 represents this concept of the overall attention by adding up all 30 attention weight vectors, with and without penalization.

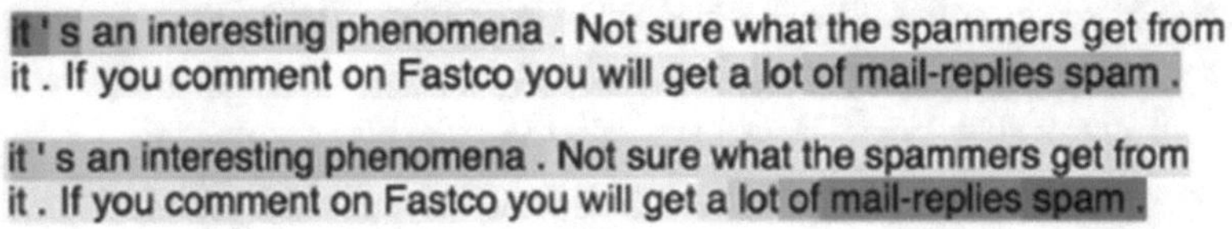

> **it's** an interesting phenomena . Not sure what the spammers get from it . If you comment on Fastco you will get a lot of mail-replies spam .

> it's an interesting phenomena . Not sure what the spammers get from it . If you comment on Fastco you will get a lot of **mail-replies spam** .

Figure 5-4. Overall attention without penalization and with 1.0 penalization

Sentiment Analysis Case

For the research paper, a Yelp dataset (`www.yelp.com/dataset_challenge`) has been selected for the sentiment analysis task. It consists of 2.7M Yelp reviews, from which 500K review-star pairs have been randomly selected as the training set, 2,000 for the development set, and 2,000 for the test set. The review is taken as input, and the number of stars is predicted in accordance with what the user has actually written for each of the reviews corresponding to the business store.

A 100-dimensional word2vec is used to initialize word embeddings, and the embeddings are further tuned during training. The target number of stars is an integer number in the range of [1,2,3,4,5], inclusive, and, thus, the task is treated as a classification task, i.e., classifying a review text into one of the five classes, and the classification accuracy is used for measurement. For the two baseline models, a batch size of 32 is used, and the hidden unit numbers in the output MLP is chosen as 3,000.

As an interpretation of the learned sentence embedding, the second way of visualization is used below, to plot the heat maps for some of the reviews in the dataset. Three reviews are selected randomly. As inferred from Figure 5-5, the model majorly learns to capture some key factors in the review that indicate strongly the sentiment behind the sentence. For most of the short reviews, the model manages to capture all the key factors that contribute to an extreme score, but for longer reviews, the model is still not able to capture all related factors. As reflected in the first review, a lot of focus is placed on one single factor, "be nothing extraordinary," and little attention is on other key points, such as "annoying thing," "so hard/cold," etc.

we have a great work dinner here there be about 20 us and the staff do a great job time the course the food be nothing extraordinary I order the New York strip the meat can have use a little more marbling the cornbread we get before the salad be the good thing I eat the whole night 1 annoying thing at this place be the butter be so hard / cold you can not use it on the soft bread get with it

this place be great for lunch / dinner happy hour too the staff be very nice and helpful my new spot

price reasonable staff - helpful attentive portion huge enough for 2 if you get the chimichanga plate food too salty as u know when you cook or add anything with cheese it have it own salt no need add more to the meat ... pls kill the salt and then you can taste the goodness of the food ... ty

we have a great work dinner here there be about 20 us and the staff do a great job time the course the food be nothing extraordinary I order the New York strip the meat can have use a little more marbling the cornbread we get before the salad be the good thing I eat the whole night 1 annoying thing at this place be the butter be so hard / cold you can not use it on the soft bread get with it

this place be great for lunch / dinner happy hour too the staff be very nice and helpful my new spot

price reasonable staff - helpful attentive portion huge enough for 2 if you get the chimichanga plate food too salty as u know when you cook or add anything with cheese it have it own salt no need add more to the meat ... pls kill the salt and then you can taste the goodness of the food ... ty

Figure 5-5. Attention of sentence embedding on three different Yelp reviews, trained without and with 1.0 penalization

Research Findings

The paper introduces a fixed size, matrix sentence embedding with a self-attention mechanism, which helps in interpreting the sentence embedding in depth in the model. Introducing the attention mechanism allows the final sentence embedding to directly access previous LSTM hidden states, via the attention summation. Thus, the LSTM doesn't have to carry every piece of information toward its last hidden state. Instead, each LSTM hidden state is only expected to provide shorter-term context information about each word, while the higher-level semantics, which requires longer term dependency, can be picked up directly by the attention mechanism. This setting relieves the burden of LSTM to carry on long-term dependencies. The notion of adding up elements in the attention mechanism is very primitive. It can be something more complex than that, which will allow more operations on the hidden states of LSTM.

The model can encode any sequence of variable length into a fixed-size representation, without suffering from long-term dependency problems. This brings a lot of scalability to the model, and without any significant modification, it can be applied directly to longer contents, such as paragraphs, articles, etc.

Implementing Sentiment Classification

We have made use of the Internet Movie Database, popularly known as IMDb (www.imdb.com), to select the dataset for the sentiment classification problem. It offers a great number of datasets, both image and text, which are useful for multiple research activities in deep learning and data analysis.

For sentiment classification, we have made use of a set of 25,000 movie reviews, which have their positive and negative label attached. The publicly available reviews have been already preprocessed and are encoded as a sequence of word indexes, i.e., integers. The words are ordered on the basis of their overall frequency in the dataset, i.e., the token or word with the second-highest frequency has been indexed as 2, and so on. Attaching such an index to the words will help in shortlisting the words on the basis of their frequency, such as to pick the top 2,000 most common words or remove the top-10 most common words. Following is code to view a sample of the training dataset.

```python
from keras.datasets import imdb
(X_train,y_train), (X_test,y_test) = imdb.load_data(num_
words=1000, index_from=3)

# Getting the word index used for encoding the sequences
vocab_to_int = imdb.get_word_index()
vocab_to_int = {k:(v+3) for k,v in vocab_to_int.items()}
# Starting from word index offset onward

# Creating indexes for the special characters : Padding, Start
Token, Unknown words
vocab_to_int["<PAD>"] = 0
vocab_to_int["<GO>"] = 1
vocab_to_int["<UNK>"] = 2

int_to_vocab = {value:key for key,value in vocab_to_int.
items()}
print(' '.join(int_to_vocab[id] for id in X_train[0] ))

>
<GO> this film was just brilliant casting <UNK> <UNK> story
direction <UNK> really <UNK> the part they played and you could
just imagine being there robert <UNK> is an amazing actor and
now the same being director <UNK> father came from the same
<UNK> <UNK> as myself so i loved the fact there was a real <UNK>
with this film the <UNK> <UNK> throughout the film were great
it was just brilliant so much that i <UNK> the film as soon as
```

it was released for <UNK> and would recommend it to everyone
to watch and the <UNK> <UNK> was amazing really <UNK> at the
end it was so sad and you know what they say if you <UNK> at a
film it must have been good and this definitely was also <UNK>
to the two little <UNK> that played the <UNK> of <UNK> and paul
they were just brilliant children are often left out of the
<UNK> <UNK> i think because the stars that play them all <UNK>
up are such a big <UNK> for the whole film but these children
are amazing and should be <UNK> for what they have done don't
you think the whole story was so <UNK> because it was true and
was <UNK> life after all that was <UNK> with us all

Sentiment Classification Code

The last section of this book covers the implementation of the concept
described in the previously mentioned paper and its use for sentiment
classification of the selected IMDb datasets. The required IMDb datasets
can be downloaded automatically from the following code. If required,
one can also download the dataset from the following URL and look at
the set of reviews available: https://s3.amazonaws.com/text-datasets/
imdb_full.pkl.

Note   Make sure you have an open Internet connection on the
machine before running the code, to enable the dataset download,
and TensorFlow version 1.3.0.

"0" has not been used to encode any word, as it is used to encode
the unknown word in the vocabulary.

Import the required packages and checking packages version, where required.

```
# Importing TensorFlow and IMDb dataset from keras library
from keras.datasets import imdb
import tensorflow as tf
> Using TensorFlow backend.
```

```
# Checking TensorFlow version
print(tf.__version__)
> 1.3.0
```

```
from __future__ import print_function
from tensorflow.python.ops import rnn, rnn_cell
import numpy as np
import pandas as pd
import matplotlib.pyplot as plt
%matplotlib inline
```

The next step is to create the train/test datasets from the reviews dataset of IMDb. Keras datasets offers a built-in function for it, which returns the following couple of tuples with the sequence and labels list:

- X_train, X_test: These are lists of sequences that have the lists of indexes, i.e., normal integers assigned to each of the words. If, while importing the dataset, the num_words argument is specified, the maximum possible index value selected is num_words-1, and if the maxlen argument is specified, then it is used to pick the largest possible sequence length.

- y_train, y_test: These are the lists of integer labels, assigned 1 or 0, for positive and negative reviews, respectively.

The `imdb.load_data()` function takes eight arguments to customize the review dataset selection. Following is a detailed explanation of these arguments:

- path: If the data is not present locally in the Keras datasets folder, it will be downloaded to the specified location.

- num_words: (Type: `integer` or None) Selects the top most frequent words to be considered for the modeling purpose. Words out of this range and with a frequency less than these will be replaced with the oov_char value in the sequence data.

- skip_top: (Type: `integer`) This skips the top most-frequent words from the selection. Such bypassed words are replaced with the oov_char value in the sequence data.

- maxlen: (Type: `int`) Used to specify the maximum length of the sequence. Sequences longer then the specified length will be truncated.

- seed: (Type: `int`) Sets the seed to reproduce the data shuffling

- start_char: (Type: `int`) This character marks the start of a sequence. It is set to 1, because 0 is usually used to pad characters.

- oov_char: (Type: int) Words cut out by the num_words or skip_top arguments will be replaced by this character.

- index_from: (Type: int) Indexes actual words and more. It is a Word indexing offset.

```
# Creating Train and Test datasets from labeled movie reviews
(X_train, y_train), (X_test, y_test) = imdb.load_
data(path="imdb_full.pkl",num_words=None, skip_top=0,
maxlen=None, seed=113, tart_char=1, oov_char=2, index_from=3)
> Downloading data from https://s3.amazonaws.com/text-datasets/
imdb.npz
```

Each of the sequences in the review set is of a length of 200, and further vocabulary has been created from the training dataset. Figure 5-6 shows the distribution of the word count in reviews.

```
X_train[:2]
> array([ list([1, 14, 22, 16, 43, 530, 973, 1622, 1385, 65,
458, 4468, 66, 3941, 4, 173, 36, 256, 5, 25, 100, 43, 838, 112,
50, 670, 22665, ....
```

```
t = [item for sublist in X_train for item in sublist]
vocabulary = len(set(t))+1
```

```
a = [len(x) for x in X_train]
plt.plot(a)
```

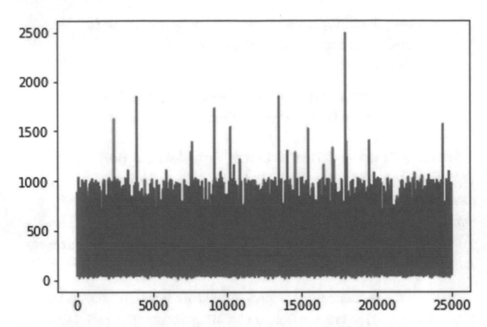

Figure 5-6. *Distribution of word counts in each of the reviews*

Specify a maximum length for the selection of a sequence from the sentence, and if the review length is lower than it, append the newly created sequence with padding, up to the maximum length.

```
max_length = 200 # specifying the max length of the sequence in
the sentence
x_filter = []
y_filter = []

# If the selected length is lesser than the specified max_
length, 200, then appending padding (0), else only selecting
desired length only from sentence
for i in range(len(X_train)):
    if len(X_train[i])<max_length:
        a = len(X_train[i])
        X_train[i] = X_train[i] + [0] * (max_length - a)
```

```
        x_filter.append(X_train[i])
        y_filter.append(y_train[i])
    elif len(X_train[i])>max_length:
        X_train[i] = X_train[i][0:max_length]
```

Declare the model hyperparameters with word embedding size, number of hidden units, learning rate, batch size, and total number of training iterations.

```
#declaring the hyper params
embedding_size = 100    # word vector size for initializing the
                          word embeddings
n_hidden = 200
learning_rate = 0.06
training_iters = 100000
batch_size = 32
beta =0.0001
```

Declare additional parameters related to the current model architecture and dataset, max_length, number of classes to classify in, number of units in hidden layer of self-attention MLP, and number of rows in matrix embedding.

```
n_steps = max_length          # timestepswords
n_classes = 2                 # 0/1 : binary classification for
                                negative and positive reviews
da = 350                      # hyper-parameter : Self-attention
                                MLP has hidden layer with da
                                units
r = 30                        # count of different parts to be
                                extracted from sentence (= number
                                of rows in matrix embedding)
display_step =10
hidden_units = 3000
```

Transform the training dataset values and labels in the desired format of array post transformation and encoding, respectively.

```
y_train = np.asarray(pd.get_dummies(y_filter))
X_train = np.asarray([np.asarray(g) for g in x_filter])
```

Create an internal folder to record logs.

```
logs_path = './recent_logs/'
```

Create a DataIterator class, to yield random data in batches of given batch size.

```
class DataIterator:
    """ Collects data and yields bunch of batches of data
    Takes data sources and batch_size as arguments """
    def __init__(self, data1,data2, batch_size):
        self.data1 = data1
        self.data2 = data2
        self.batch_size = batch_size
        self.iter = self.make_random_iter()

    def next_batch(self):
        try:
            idxs = next(self.iter)
        except StopIteration:
            self.iter = self.make_random_iter()
            idxs = next(self.iter)
        X =[self.data1[i] for i in idxs]
        Y =[self.data2[i] for i in idxs]

        X = np.array(X)
        Y = np.array(Y)
        return X, Y
```

```python
def make_random_iter(self):
    splits = np.arange(self.batch_size, len(self.data1),
    self.batch_size)
    it = np.split(np.random.permutation(range(len(self.
    data1))), splits)[:-1]
    return iter(it)
```

Initialize weights and biases and input placeholders in the next step. The general rule for setting the weights in a neural network is to be close to zero, without being too small. A good practice is to start your weights in the range of $[-y, y]$, where $y = 1/\sqrt{n}$ (n is the number of inputs to a given neuron).

```python
############## Graph Creation ################

# TF Graph Input
with tf.name_scope("weights"):
    Win  = tf.Variable(tf.random_uniform([n_hidden*r, hidden_
    units],-1/np.sqrt(n_hidden),1/np.sqrt(n_hidden)), name=
    'W-input')
    Wout = tf.Variable(tf.random_uniform([hidden_units,
    n_classes],-1/np.sqrt(hidden_units),1/np.sqrt(hidden_
    units)), name='W-out')
    Ws1  = tf.Variable(tf.random_uniform([da,n_hidden],-1/
    np.sqrt(da),1/np.sqrt(da)), name='Ws1')
    Ws2  = tf.Variable(tf.random_uniform([r,da],-1/
    np.sqrt(r),1/np.sqrt(r)), name='Ws2')

with tf.name_scope("biases"):
    biasesout = tf.Variable(tf.random_normal([n_classes]),
    name='biases-out')
    biasesin  = tf.Variable(tf.random_normal([hidden_units]),
    name='biases-in')
```

```
with tf.name_scope('input'):
    x = tf.placeholder("int32", [32,max_length], name=
    'x-input')
    y = tf.placeholder("int32", [32, 2], name='y-input')
```

Create tensors in the same default graph context with the embedded vectors. This takes the embedding matrix and an input tensor, such as the review vectors.

```
with tf.name_scope('embedding'):
    embeddings = tf.Variable(tf.random_uniform([vocabulary,
    embedding_size],-1, 1), name='embeddings')
    embed = tf.nn.embedding_lookup(embeddings,x)
```

```
def length(sequence):
    # Computing maximum of elements across dimensions of a
    tensor
    used = tf.sign(tf.reduce_max(tf.abs(sequence), reduction_
    indices=2))

    length = tf.reduce_sum(used, reduction_indices=1)
    length = tf.cast(length, tf.int32)
    return length
```

Reuse the weights and biases using the following:

```
with tf.variable_scope('forward',reuse=True):
        lstm_fw_cell = rnn_cell.BasicLSTMCell(n_hidden)
```

```
with tf.name_scope('model'):
    outputs, states = rnn.dynamic_rnn(lstm_fw_
    cell,embed,sequence_length=length(embed),dtype=tf.
    float32,time_major=False)
    # in the next step we multiply the hidden-vec matrix with
    the Ws1 by reshaping
```

```python
h = tf.nn.tanh(tf.transpose(tf.reshape(tf.
matmul(Ws1,tf.reshape(outputs,[n_hidden,batch_size*n_
steps])),  [da,batch_size,n_steps]),[1,0,2]))
# in this step we multiply the generated matrix with Ws2
a = tf.reshape(tf.matmul(Ws2,tf.reshape(h,[da,batch_size*n_
steps])),[batch_size,r,n_steps])
def fn3(a,x):
        return tf.nn.softmax(x)
h3 = tf.scan(fn3,a)
with tf.name_scope('flattening'):
    # here we again multiply(batch) of the generated batch with
    the same hidden matrix
    h4 = tf.matmul(h3,outputs)
    # flattening the output embedded matrix
    last = tf.reshape(h4,[-1,r*n_hidden])

with tf.name_scope('MLP'):
    tf.nn.dropout(last,.5, noise_shape=None, seed=None,
    name=None)
    pred1 = tf.nn.sigmoid(tf.matmul(last,Win)+biasesin)
    pred  = tf.matmul(pred1, Wout) + biasesout

# Define loss and optimizer
with tf.name_scope('cross'):
    cost = tf.reduce_mean(tf.nn.softmax_cross_entropy_with_
    logits(logits =pred, labels = y) + beta*tf.nn.l2_loss(Ws2) )

with tf.name_scope('train'):
    optimizer = tf.train.AdamOptimizer(learning_rate=learning_
    rate)
    gvs = optimizer.compute_gradients(cost)
    capped_gvs = [(tf.clip_by_norm(grad,0.5), var) for grad,
    var in gvs]
```

```
    optimizer.apply_gradients(capped_gvs)
    optimized = optimizer.minimize(cost)

# Evaluate model
with tf.name_scope('Accuracy'):
    correct_pred = tf.equal(tf.argmax(pred,1), tf.argmax(y,1))
    accuracy     = tf.reduce_mean(tf.cast(correct_pred,
    tf.float32))

tf.summary.scalar("cost", cost)
tf.summary.scalar("accuracy", accuracy)
> <tf.Tensor 'accuracy:0' shape=() dtype=string>

# merge all summaries into a single "summary operation" which
we can execute in a session
summary_op =tf.summary.merge_all()
# Initializing the variables
train_iter = DataIterator(X_train,y_train, batch_size)
init = tf.global_variables_initializer()

# This could give warning if in case the required port is being
used already
# Running the command again or releasing the port before the
subsequent run should solve the purpose
```

Start to train the model. Make sure the batch_size is sufficient enough to fit system requirements.

```
with tf.Session() as sess:
    sess.run(init)
    # Creating log file writer object
    writer = tf.summary.FileWriter(logs_path, graph=tf.get_
    default_graph())
    step = 1
```

```python
# Keep training until reach max iterations
while step * batch_size < training_iters:
    batch_x, batch_y = train_iter.next_batch()
    sess.run(optimized, feed_dict={x: batch_x, y: batch_y})
    # Executing the summary operation in the session
    summary = sess.run(summary_op, feed_dict={x: batch_x,
    y: batch_y})
    # Writing the values in log file using the FileWriter
    object created above
    writer.add_summary(summary,  step*batch_size)
    if step % display_step == 2:
        # Calculate batch accuracy
        acc = sess.run(accuracy, feed_dict={x: batch_x, y:
        batch_y})
        # Calculate batch loss
        loss = sess.run(cost, feed_dict={x: batch_x, y:
        batch_y})
        print ("Iter " + str(step*batch_size) + ",
                Minibatch Loss= " + "{:.6f}".format(loss)
                + ", Training Accuracy= " + "{:.2f}".
                format(acc*100) + "%")

    step += 1
print ("Optimization Finished!")
```

```
> Iter 64, Minibatch Loss= 68.048653, Training Accuracy= 50.00%
> Iter 384, Minibatch Loss= 69.634018, Training Accuracy= 53.12%
> Iter 704, Minibatch Loss= 50.814949, Training Accuracy= 46.88%
> Iter 1024, Minibatch Loss= 39.475891, Training Accuracy= 56.25%
> Iter 1344, Minibatch Loss= 11.115482, Training Accuracy= 40.62%
> Iter 1664, Minibatch Loss= 7.060193, Training Accuracy= 59.38%
```

```
> Iter 1984, Minibatch Loss= 2.565218, Training Accuracy= 43.75%
> Iter 2304, Minibatch Loss= 18.036911, Training Accuracy= 46.88%
> Iter 2624, Minibatch Loss= 18.796995, Training Accuracy= 43.75%
> Iter 2944, Minibatch Loss= 56.627518, Training Accuracy= 43.75%
> Iter 3264, Minibatch Loss= 29.162407, Training Accuracy= 43.75%
> Iter 3584, Minibatch Loss= 14.335728, Training Accuracy= 40.62%
> Iter 3904, Minibatch Loss= 1.863467, Training Accuracy= 53.12%
> Iter 4224, Minibatch Loss= 7.892468, Training Accuracy= 50.00%
> Iter 4544, Minibatch Loss= 4.554517, Training Accuracy= 53.12%

> Iter 95744, Minibatch Loss= 28.283163, Training Accuracy= 59.38%
> Iter 96064, Minibatch Loss= 1.305542, Training Accuracy= 50.00%
> Iter 96384, Minibatch Loss= 1.801988, Training Accuracy= 50.00%
> Iter 96704, Minibatch Loss= 1.896597, Training Accuracy= 53.12%
> Iter 97024, Minibatch Loss= 2.941552, Training Accuracy= 46.88%
> Iter 97344, Minibatch Loss= 0.693964, Training Accuracy= 56.25%
> Iter 97664, Minibatch Loss= 8.340314, Training Accuracy= 40.62%
> Iter 97984, Minibatch Loss= 2.635653, Training Accuracy= 56.25%
> Iter 98304, Minibatch Loss= 1.541869, Training Accuracy= 68.75%
> Iter 98624, Minibatch Loss= 1.544908, Training Accuracy= 62.50%
> Iter 98944, Minibatch Loss= 26.138868, Training Accuracy= 56.25%
> Iter 99264, Minibatch Loss= 17.603979, Training Accuracy= 56.25%
> Iter 99584, Minibatch Loss= 21.715031, Training Accuracy= 40.62%
> Iter 99904, Minibatch Loss= 17.485657, Training Accuracy= 53.12%
> Optimization Finished!
```

Model Results

The modeling results have been recorded using the TensorFlow summaries, or logs, and saved while running the model script. To write the logs, log writer `FileWriter()` has been used, which internally creates the log folder and saves the graph structure. The recorded summary operations are later used by TensorBoard for visualization purposes. We have saved the logs at the following internal folder location of the current working directory: `logs_path = './recent_logs/'`.

To start the TensorBoard, specify the port, per your choice: `tensorboard --logdir=./ --port=6006`.

TensorBoard

To make the TensorBoard visualization more readable, we have added the name for placeholders and variables, wherever required. TensorBoard helps in debugging and optimization of the code.

We have added the graph of the overall model and a few of its segments, to help in relating the code with the TensorFlow graph visual. All the segments are relatable with their corresponding code segments in the previous subsection.

Figure 5-7 shows the full network architecture for the sentiment classification. The graph shows the variables that have been scoped throughout the code, which helps in understanding the flow of the data and connections across the model.

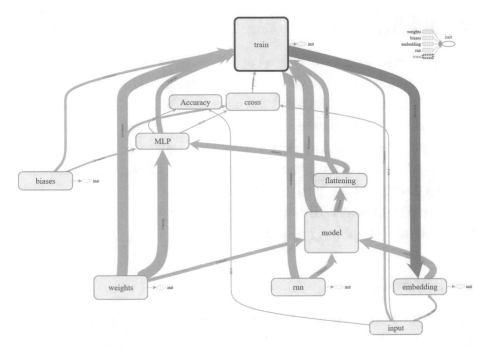

Figure 5-7. *TensorFlow graph of the overall model*

Figure 5-8 shows the MLP component of the graph, which is used to add the addition of dropout to the last layer, and the sigmoid function to predict the final sentiment classification results. The final predictions are further used to gather the model's accuracy and cost.

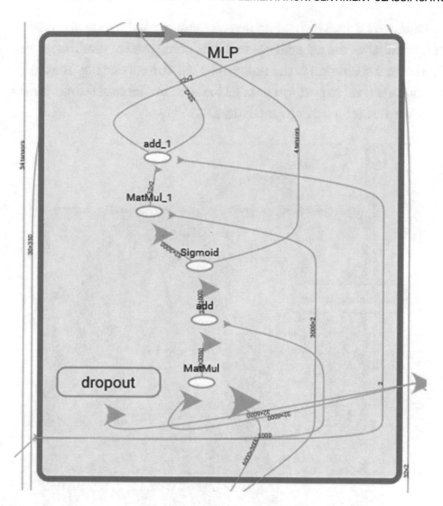

Figure 5-8. *TensorBoard graph for the MLP segment*

Figure 5-9 shows the *embedding* component of the network. It is used to initialize the embeddings variable, composed of random values of uniform distribution in the range of [-1,1). The embedding_lookup() technique is used to perform parallel lookups on the embeddings tensor, which are further used as input to the LSTM layer.

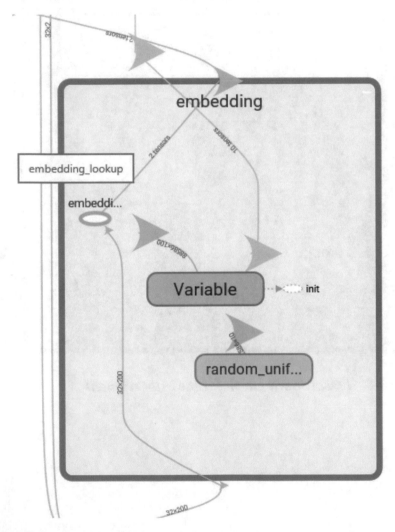

Figure 5-9. *TensorBoard graph for the embedding segment*

Model Accuracy and Cost

Following are the model accuracy and cost graphs for the four simulations performed on the IMDb dataset and for two cases with different smoothing filter parameter values.

Note   A smoothing filter is used in TensorBoard as a weighing parameter that controls the window size. A weight of 1.0 means using 50 percent of the entire dataset as the window, while a weight of 0.0 means using a window of 0 (and, thus, replacing each point with itself). The filter acts as an additional parameter to interpret graphs thoroughly.

Case 1

For the first case, the smoothing filter value has been set as 0.191, and we have compared the model accuracy and cost over four different simulations (Figures 5-10 and 5-11).

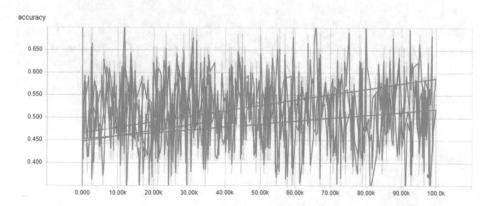

Figure 5-10.   *TensorBoard graph for the accuracy parameter*

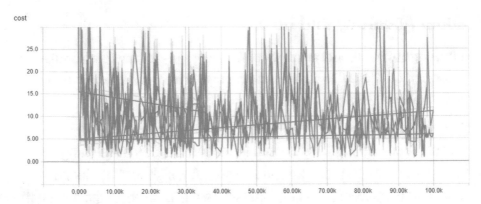

Figure 5-11. *TensorBoard graph for the cost parameter*

Case 2

For the second case, the smoothing value has been set as 0.645, and we have compared the model accuracy and cost over four different simulations (Figures 5-12 and 5-13).

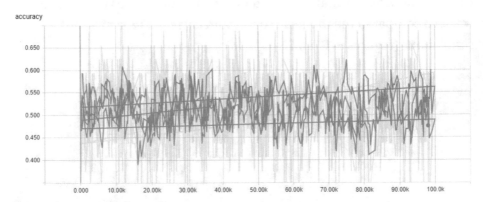

Figure 5-12. *TensorBoard graph for accuracy parameter*

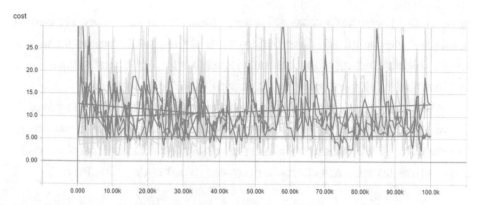

Figure 5-13. *TensorBoard graph for cost parameter*

Scope for Improvement

As inferred from the preceding graphs, the model accuracy is not significantly great and reaches close to 70 percent in some cases. There are a few ways by which the results achieved from the preceding exercise could be further improved, by making variations in the training data fed to the model and by refining the hyperparameters of the model. The training dataset used for sentiment analysis in the paper comprises 500K of Yelp reviews and rest for development and test purposes. In the exercise performed, we have taken 25K reviews. To further improve the model's performance, readers are invited to make changes in the code and compare the results of multiple iterations. The changes made to improve the results should be in accordance with the values mentioned in the paper, thereby helping in the comparison of results across multiple datasets.

Next Steps

This last chapter of the book presented the implementation of a chosen research paper's sentiment analysis. We would like readers of all backgrounds to carry out such activities and attempt to replicate, on their chosen datasets in their preferred languages, the algorithms and approaches presented across different papers and conferences. We believe such exercises heighten the understanding of the research papers and widen understanding of the different types of algorithms that can be applied to the relevant datasets for solving specific problems.

We hope readers have enjoyed the journey through all the use cases featured in this book. We would be very grateful to them for suggestions to improve the quality of the code and theory presented herein, and we will ensure that any relevant changes are made in our code repository.

Index

A

Activation potential, 40
Annotated corpus
  add padding, 162
  check versions, 158
  create checkpoints, 164, 166
  create input, 160
  create train and validation
    datasets, 163
  dropout, 163
  DRUG-AE.rel file, 160
  embedding file, 159
  import modules, 158
  Keras modules, 163
  LSTM network, 164
  performance, 166–167
  text file, 159–160
  time distributed
    layers, 163
  validation dataset, 166
Artificial neural network
  (ANN), 36–37
  backpropagation
    mechanism, 59
Attention scoring
  network, 152–155

B

Backpropagation algorithm, 57–60
Backpropagation through time
  (BPTT), 136
Bag-of-word models, 76
Bidirectional encoders, 148–149
Binary sequence summation, 135
Blood transfusion dataset, 70–73

C

Chatbots
  building, 174
  definition, 18, 169–170
  Facebook (*see* Facebook,
    chatbot)
  higher level, 172–173
  insurance dataset (*see*
    Insurance QnA dataset)
  origin of, 170–171
  platforms, 174
  working, 172
Continuous bag-of-words (CBOW)
  model, 81
  AdaGrad optimizer, 112–113
  architecture, 87

© Palash Goyal, Sumit Pandey, Karan Jain 2018
P. Goyal, et al., *Deep Learning for Natural Language Processing*,
https://doi.org/10.1007/978-1-4842-3685-7

Y, Z

Printed in the United States
By Bookmasters